READY STEADY GO!

GROWING UP IN THE FIFTIES AND SIXTIES

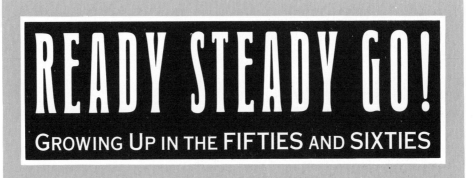

READY STEADY GO!

GROWING UP IN THE FIFTIES AND SIXTIES

CHRIS TARRANT

ADDITIONAL MATERIAL BY

CHRISTY CAMPBELL AND IAN MORRISON

PYRAMID BOOKS

PYRAMID BOOKS

First published 1990
Pyramid Books is an imprint of Octopus Illustrated Publishing,
Michelin House, 81 Fulham Road, London SW3 6RB
part of Reed International Books.

Reprinted 1991

The Author's moral rights have been asserted.

A catalogue record for this book is
available from the British Library.

ISBN 1 855 100223

Produced by Mandarin Offset
Printed and bound in Hong Kong

CONTENTS

Ready Steady Go!

GROWING UP IN THE FIFTIES AND SIXTIES

So what do I remember about the fifties and sixties? Much the same as everyone else who grew up at that time I suspect. There was an austere drabness and greyness about our little world; there was none of the hectic colour that was to become so much a part of the seventies. Buildings were old and mainly built of dark red brick. There were no towering skyscrapers reflecting the sunlight, no neon signs, no bright supermarkets. Shops were rather dark and poorly lit by today's standards, although the service was much more attentive, much more personal.

We lived in Reading and I remember being dragged round and round the place by my Mum, and nice men and ladies in the shops giving me free sweets and apples. This did nothing to change my absolute loathing of all shopping everywhere, but at least filled my mouth up for a few precious minutes, stopping me whingeing on and on, 'Are we finished yet?' or 'Isn't it time to catch the trolley bus home?' We had walked for what seemed like at least 30 miles to catch the bus (it was actually about 300 yards) and then walked at least another 50 miles before catching the trolley back to Liverpool Road and trudging back home again. My step was always lighter on this last lap because the whole dreadful business was nearly over, while Mum's was considerably more heavily weighed down with a large shopping bag full of things like *Campcoffee* and big packets of *Rinso* and *Oxydol*. If she picked up some cigarettes for Dad they were probably *Senior Service* and if

I'd been particularly good, which was rare, at the bottom of the basket there'd be some *Spangles*.

You could still buy cigarettes in fives with names like *Black Cat, Craven 'A', Gold Flake* and *Turf*, and although my father hasn't smoked now for something like 20 years, I can still remember as a little boy peering through the haze in our living room just praying that his mate's *Woodbine* would end soon.

If Mum didn't mind walking to the bus stop, Dad and Grandad actually loved walking everywhere. It was my grandfather, still going strong today at the ripe old age of 96, who walked the most. His idea of 'a good walk' was about 30 miles long. He's always lived near Reading in open countryside, often in the middle of absolutely nowhere. If he fancied a day's fishing at, say, Newbury on the River Kennet, about 15 or 16 miles away, he'd get up before sunrise and walk there. And if Dad and I couldn't invent some perfectly reasonable excuse like a sudden recurrence of anthrax or a broken leg, we'd have to go too. Grandad's extraordinary physical stamina was presumably a great help to him when he suddenly decided to get married again at the age of 85.

Compared to Grandad my father was an also ran in the walking stakes. He would do nothing more demanding than walk to work every day, a distance of probably no more than five or six miles. From the age of five until I went away to school at the age of 13, Dad and I were a familiar sight as he dropped me off at school on his way to work — striding manfully ahead, dragging me behind.

At primary school the teachers, like everything else, were shrouded in dark, dull colours. To a man — or woman — they were very strict and had a great fondness for hitting children, particularly me. The cane was a regular feature of my schooldays, and I was hit around the back of the head daily. There was no question of complaining or your parents taking legal action against them. It was just what teachers did to revolting little irks like me, and you most certainly didn't tell anybody when you got home, or you got into further trouble.

We wore grey uniforms, with grey shorts, grey socks, grey ears, grey necks, and grey Viyella shirts. My mother was fanatical about my appearance and had me turned out in a freshly washed and ironed Viyella shirt every single morning. When I went away to school and had to look after myself, I discovered that a good Viyella shirt could last over three and a half weeks. I only used to change them when all the other little Lord Fauntleroys started to noticeably avoid me and the flies above me started throwing themselves on their own swords . . .

THE BROWN SUIT BRIGADE

To do any job of work it seemed you had to have a dark suit. Ladies in shops wore grey suits or grey overalls and pop stars wore blue suits and ties with shiny plastic shoes and hair smarmed down with chip fat. If teenagers went to a 'hop' on a Saturday night, after a whole week of wearing a grey, black or — daringly — brown suit to their new job, they'd have a bath, spend four hours *Brylcreem*ing and brushing their hair, and then put on another suit.

All the major record shops had music booths where you could listen to the likes of Tommy Steele before being thrown out for not buying anything.

Hairstyles among my mates were pretty much identical: short. At the time we were convinced that our styles were rebelliously shaggy, but in point of fact by the standards of the decades to follow, they were anything but. We were all dragged off to the barber's about once a fortnight, where signs like 'No Styles, No Trims' were nailed up over the mirror, and you had a choice of short back and sides, or very short back and sides; there was usually no attempt at tapering, you just had great steps cut up the side of your head, with optional singeing as the only extra refinement. Singeing was basically something that barbers did to the end of your new mown hair with a lighted candle. To this day I've no idea what it was supposed to achieve. It's probably based on the same principle as setting wheat or sugar cane alight just after it's been cut to flush out the rats and resting cobras.

Anyway we went through this ritual every couple of weeks, plastered down the burnt remains with *Trugel* or *Brylcreem* and convinced ourselves we looked like Adam Faith or this spotty little new bloke called Cliff Richard.

Music was nothing like the unavoidable part of all our lives that it is now, but by the end of the fifties it was clear that something was changing. My early memories of music at home were of Dad singing *Once On a High Windy Hill* in the bathroom every morning for about nine years, and Jimmy Young having a hit with *Man From Laramie*. Even at an early age I knew that this song was dreadful, an opinion I've never revised. Most of Dad's limited collection of records were by Frank Sinatra and Bing Crosby. Mum was a bit of a secret Johnny Ray fan, I vaguely recall, but I don't think it was the sort of thing you were allowed to admit in polite society. It put you on a par with girls who wore short socks to go out of an evening to Johnny Ray concerts and swoon and make a nasty mess on the seat they'd been given in the theatre when he sang something about *A Little White Cloud That Cried*. There'd apparently been a bit of this sort of nonsense with the young Frank Sinatra, and Johnny Ray and Frankie Vaughan seemed to have the same sort of effect on young girls with fast developing anatomies. But it was nothing like what was to come with Beatlemania, Stonemania, Monkeymania etc. etc. on through the decades ad infinitum. Everything that just began to cause a slight ripple in the late fifties was to burst into full flood inside the next ten years.

THE REIGN OF THE DANSETTE *MAJOR*

At the end of the fifties we were all just about beginning to update our gramophones for something altogether more hi-tech, the Dansette *Major* record player. For years we'd managed perfectly happily on our wind-up handled gramophones, with a large horn as the speaker and a little tin of sharp-pointed steel needles. You screwed them into the very heavy music head and only changed them when they were really blunt. This didn't usually take very long. As all records were played at 78 revolutions per minute, the delicate needles were reduced to nothing after just a few quick bursts of *Man From Laramie*.

Choosing records was a serious business — I ought to say it still is for me. Aided by a Dansette, listening to music became a full-time occupation.

The legendary state of the art Dansette *Major* (or *Minor* for the less well endowed with pocket or paper round money) was to change the playing of records for ever. For starters it had one extra strong needle actually wired into the music playing head. What a breakthrough. No more hunting around on the carpet with a torch at parties to try and find the only needle that wasn't blunt so the dancing could recommence. This was a brave new dawn of advanced technology. Not only that, but you could actually play more than one record at a time. You could pile them up one on top of the other in the middle so that they would play in turn without you having to keep racing back to the gramophone to put on another one right in the middle of a particularly rivetting chat about the *Eagle* club, or something incredibly funny you'd heard Uncle Mac say on 'Childrens' Hour'. Uncle Mac of course was a legend. He'd have been a Disc Jockey, only I don't think anybody had invented them then. He was really called Derek McCulloch and used to do a hugely successful show for children on the wireless every Saturday morning. He basically had about five records that he used to play every week, whether you wanted him to or not. One was something to do with a 'goat-eating troll that lived under a bridge' somewhere in Scandinavia, another was about a 'man who swallowed a horse, he's dead of course', and all the rest of the playlist were by Danny Kaye. Even as a small child I knew that Uncle Mac had all the charisma of a dung beetle. He did have a couple of wacky catch phrases: 'Hallo Children', that was one, and the other was, as quick as a flash, 'Hallo Twins' whenever two children he was droningly saying hallo to between Danny Kaye records had the same name, address, age and birthday. Sharp as a marble was Uncle Mac. However, he had a good run on prime time British radio, before legends like Ed Stewart, with his even wackier catchphrase of 'Morning', and Tony 'Not Now Arnold' Blackburn took over the same request slot years later, still presumably working with Dansette *Majors* and *Minors*.

MOVIES IN THE HOME

Radio seems to be coming back into fashion in the nineties, as the ever less satisfying fare offered by an increasing number of TV stations is finding smaller and smaller audiences, but certainly in the fifties radio was a major part of family lives. Nor did there seem to be much differentiation between what was for growing kids and what was for grown-ups. As a family we listened to Billy Cotton, a man of at least 100 who did a band show every Sunday with the unforgettably named Greesha Farfell (I think) on trumpet. Sunday lunchtime radio was a major family event in most households. For the kids it was Sunday school in the morning then home to Billy and

Greesha, probably just catching the end of 'Two Way Family Favourites' with Bill Crozier and Jean McDonald and then either the hugely popular Tony Hancock in 'Hancock's Half Hour', or 'Educating Archie'.

'Educating Archie' starred Peter Brough, Archie Andrews and the young, lissom Beryl Reid. Beryl of course has gone on from eccentric strength to strength, but Peter

and Archie haven't been heard of for some time. In all events, however, they had an amazingly good run for what seemed at the time the perfectly acceptable idea of a radio ventriloquist act. Archie was a wooden dummy, Pete was the radio vent, and every Sunday we sat there impressed that we couldn't hear his lips move.

Television was becoming increasingly popular by the end of the fifties, no doubt helped in its popularity by a lack of interest in radio ventriloquism, and the new-fangled commercial television was getting a foothold in our world. There were programmes like 'Coronation Street', starring such legendary characters as Ena Sharples, Martha Longhurst and Concepta Hewitt. And there was 'Criss Cross Quiz', Eamonn Andrews doing 'Crackerjack', Michael Miles doing 'Take Your Pick' and a very young Shaw Taylor hosting an extraordinary show called 'Double Dotto', a far cry from 'Keep 'em Peeled'. At the end of the fifties colour telly was only just being thought of and people who did have TV with both BBC and ITV only had black and white sets. Sometimes sitting at home in the nineties looking at one of Noel Edmonds' jumpers or Oliver Reed's eyeballs I still wish I had black and white.

Some of the posher houses had a 'colour painting screen' that you put in front of your set to give the programmes the illusion of colour. It worked fine on programmes with sunny skies, lines of trees and nicely laid out lawns, but the same colour painting screen imposed over 'Coronation Street' meant that everyone had bright blue sunny hair and green teeth.

The other refinement which the house nextdoor to us went in for very briefly, was a 'programme enlarger'. This was a giant magnifying glass on a stand which you put in the centre of your front room half way between the sofa and the television set and everything could be viewed at treble the size of your tiny set. A three-times-as-big Albert Tatlock with bright blue sunny hair and green teeth wasn't a whole barrel of fun, but in any case this thing was equally inoperable as only about one and a half people in the family could view at the full magnified size. The rest had to make do with a sort of hall of funny mirror effect as they tried desperately to peer through the sides of the magnifying glass. The other drawback with the programme enlarger was that everybody in the family was guaranteed a vicious headache in less than 20 minutes.

Television in those early days was a very sedate affair. People were all terribly polite to each other and to us the viewers. They dressed nicely and spoke even more nicely. They had names like MacDonald Hobley, Sylvia Peters, Peter Noble and Peter Dimmock. They had nice hair cuts and clean shoes, and if anything went wrong they went bright scarlet — well bright grey anyway. Things went wrong most of the time so they often went scarlet/grey — unless you had a colour painting screen, then their faces when deeper blue and their teeth extra grass-green.

Away from the joys of Sylvia Peters, radio ventriloquists, 'Muffin the Mule' and 'The Goon Show', ours was a simple little world. I suppose we had a vague awareness that there were a few people somewhere in the Big Wide World who had pots of money, but Mum and Dad seemed to have enough for our needs, and there was none of the wall-to-wall parading of other people's wealth, life styles, cars and women that create such a sense of frustration and jealousy in so many people today.

Television gradually became a much less sedate affair with programmes like 'Ready Steady Go!' But radio never lost its appeal.

TRAIN SPOTTERS' PARADISE LOST

Friday was always the day we rushed home from school to get down by the railway track as early as possible, but definitely not later than about ten past four. Around that time the train that they'd been working on all that week further up the line at Swindon repair sheds was sent for its first test run along the main Great Western Railway line to Paddington. A Friday afternoon was also the time when Swindon released something much more revolutionary: the first of the new diesel trains. This was a real breakthrough. After years of us kids getting covered in coal dust and soot every time a steam train thundered past, these new-fangled diesels went by with no fuss whatsoever. They were noiseless and smokeless. They were also incredibly boring to look at. Most of the ones that came out of Swindon in those first diesel days are already on the scrap-heap and their widespread introduction meant the end of any individuality on the railways, and the end of my trainspotting. Within a year my Ian Allan *Bumper Book of Trainspotting* went off to a jumble sale.

The other big event that happened every Friday was Dad coming home with the bag of broken biscuits. Reading was very much a biscuit town. Dad worked for a company that supplied the tins for Huntley and Palmers to put all their biccies in. Eventually he was to become their Managing Director but at this time he was something like Head of Paper Clips, and our free bag of reject broken biscuits every Friday night was definitely a perk. After tea it was always quite a ritual as Mum shared out the cracked bits of ginger nuts and custard creams, some of which my little gang of quite revolting mates and I would scoff at once, and the rest I'd save for Saturday morning fishing.

FISHY TALES

Fishing was then a religion for the men in our family. Grandad had fished all his life, and his Grandad before him, and my Dad had me sitting beside (and occasionally in) the River Thames with my own little cane rod from the age of four. We fished the Thames at Sonning and the River Kennet at Newbury. The rivers were altogether cleaner than they are now and there was hardly any boat traffic. Our methods and fishing tackle were crude, but in those days the fish were under none of the relentless pressure from millions of fishermen that they are now, and considering our lack of skill we caught a lot of fish. Mostly they were returned to the river although occasionally my Dad would proudly push me home on my bicycle with a fat pike tied to my cross bar. The unfortunate pikes would inevitably end up chucked to the local cats. Sometimes, under pressure from Dad and I, Mum would try to cook one of these muddy creatures and invariably, for all my

Mum shared out Huntley and Palmers biscuits every Friday, some of which me and my mates would wolf down, and the rest I'd keep for Saturday's fishing trip.

mother's cooking skills, they would taste like a boiled blanket. On those nights the local cats had to wait a little longer but eventually they had a rare cooked tea thrown over the fence instead of the usual raw one.

As soon as I could swim properly my parents let me go fishing either with schoolfriends or, often, on my own. It's interesting that my parents, who were very strict and perhaps over protective even to a little eight-year-old, were

quite happy to let me go wandering off miles from the house on my bike to fish in the middle of absolutely nowhere, whereas they were constantly giving me warnings about not talking to funny men in the centre of town, or never walking home alone from school. The point was that even strict parents thought bad things happened in towns, never in the country where of course nothing ever did.

There was little crime to speak of, and very little contact with policemen at all. Most people only really met the friendly bobbies when they started to drive motor cars. At the end of the fifties the car was still something of a rarity. My Grandad had one, for all his love of walking, and we used to pile into it on Sundays in summer to go to the seaside at West Wittering. I remember one nearly fatal journey home, when the crabs that I'd spent all day collecting from rock pools and was sneaking home in a bucket with a cloth over it, somehow got out and ran up Grandad's leg as he was doing an unthinkable 50 miles an hour in his Austin A40. Having narrowly avoided catastrophe, the poor crabs were hurled out to fend for themselves, bucket and all, on Petersfield Common and I got a well-deserved thick ear.

There were no meters, no double or even single yellow lines, no traffic wardens. And I still remember sometime around 1954 or '55, three of us running to the end of the road in the middle of Reading to see a black man pass by.

So much has changed in three decades. My grandfather retired from work over 30 years ago. He grew up in the Boer War, fought through World War One and saw both his sons come home from the Second World War. At the ripe old age of 60 he must have thought he'd seen it all. Yet, still very much alive 36 years later, he can hardly believe how much the times are still changing every single week. When he retired in 1959 you could buy a large detached four-bedroomed house in Reading for around £800.

As the sixties dawned, many of the seeds for change had already been sown. The squeaky clean image of crooners like Pat Boone in the States and the wholesome chirpy cockneyness of Tommy Steele in the UK had been exposed as the pap that it was by the raunchy lyrics, and the unmistakeably genital gyrations of Elvis Presley. Rock 'n' Roll changed the world. My little Dansette *Major* was still played until it got as white hot as ever, but instead of the easily breakable 78s I bought vinyl 45s, and the steel rod in the centre was loaded up with Elvis, the Everly Brothers, Del Shannon, Buddy Holly and Billy Fury, who I thought I looked strikingly similar to. Strangely this striking similarity was never noticed by anybody else.

By now the only way to keep my trusty Dansette *Major* playing at the right speed and without jumping, was with two heavy old pennies *Scotch* taped to the back of the stylus. As I arrived in 1960 at my new room in my boarding school, the remarkably resilient little record player was one of the main attractions of my ever popular room. That and the fact I had the only toaster that didn't electrocute people.

So there we were, a bunch of scruffy 13-year-old boys, away from home for the first time somewhere in deepest Worcestershire, huddled round our toaster and Dansette *Major*. We'd been packed off by our mums and dads, presumably in the vague hope that we would re-appear in four years time as total Hooray Henries, ready to lead the country. In fact, in the main, we re-appeared in four years as the first fruits of a youth revolution which was to happen in various forms all over the western world during the next ten years. We grew our hair as long as a minor public school would allow. If we cut it at all we probably did it ourselves. I remember my Dad coming to see me one Sunday and looking at me in horrified disbelief as I emerged sporting a crazed Rasputin-style, done in the dormitory the night before with Haggis McLauchlan's nail scissors. I thought I looked fabulous. Dad thought I looked an absolute pillock. On mature reflection I think Dad's assessment was closest.

Fashion wise, things were changing at the most extraordinary pace. A Worcestershire school was hardly the place to try and keep up with what was happening on the streets of the big cities, but what was very clear was that people didn't wear suits and ties to go to the Saturday hop any more. For starters the hop itself was rapidly disappearing. Someone somewhere had discovered that young kids were actually prepared to pay money to go along to the village hall and listen to someone playing records at them. This is so much a part of all our lives now but then it was unthinkable and, to our parents, absolutely ridiculous. Why I, with my own collection of 45s and a Dansette *Major*, should pay good money to go along and listen to someone else playing us records on his slightly louder Dansette *Major* was incomprehensible, but of course it was a place to meet, a place of our own. The venues we went to in Worcester in the early sixties were hardly Stringfellows, but they were the crude forerunners of our now ubiquitous discotheques.

If our parents thought we were raving mad to pay to listen to records in public, the music we were starting to pay to hear was even further beyond their understanding. Nice cuddly Cliff Richard, Bobby Vee, Ricky Nelson, all these wholesome figures were abruptly discarded as strange rumblings came down from Liverpool. Even the gyrating Elvis became that 'nice clean man from America' compared to the mop topped fab four and all their Liverpool satellites — the Merseybeats, Gerry and the Pacemakers, the Swinging Blue Jeans, Billy J Kramer and the Searchers. My parents were just about getting over the shock of seeing John, Paul, George and Ringo's pictures all over my bedroom, and Beatles records everywhere they looked (I think for about nine years I bought every single record they made), when, as my chin began the first eruptions of adolescence, in came my new, much spottier clutch of heroes. There was the Pretty Things (possibly the ugliest band ever to walk this earth), the heavily-pimpled Paul Jones of the enormously successful Manfred Mann group, the even spottier, and far less pretty, Eric Burdon of the Animals. And then there was probably the greatest, and certainly the dirtiest and ugliest, rock and roll band of all time, the Rolling Stones. These days between tours they seem to live almost like gentlemen farmers, but when they first appeared in the sixties they were the final confirmation of everything my parent's generation thought — that their children were going completely mad. The music was loud and tuneless, the lyrics were inaudible and almost certainly filthy, and the singer was the most hideous man on earth. But in the privacy of our room with the toaster, or home for the holidays, we loved him. I quickly shifted my allegiance from the Beatles to the

Whether you were at home or at college, John, Paul, George and Ringo came with you. No point in keeping your room tidy when daydreams with your heroes were transporting you elsewhere.

Stones, and would stroll around with my lips in a perpetual pout and move with what I believed to be a rhythm 'n' blues groovy walk. In hindsight I looked more like a penguin that had swallowed a sink plunger, but I thought I looked terrific.

Trainspotting had become but a memory, and even fishing took a bit of a back seat for the next few years, although I still used to fish every Sunday morning in the summer term. Two of us were allowed to fish a small lake in the grounds of Worcester Golf Course. We would drag ourselves out of bed every Sunday at about half past three in the morning to cycle through the silent, still cobbled, streets out to the edge of town. There we'd fish happily till eight o'clock, when the early golfers would arrive, start shouting 'Look out there!' and pepper the water with golf balls. In the early days we used to pretend to help them look, then collect the lost balls up to sell later after the golfers had given up hope and moved on to the next tee. But after a couple of very near misses, one of which went only about six inches from my school cap with my head still inside it, we decided to call it best.

For a couple of summers the fishing was fabulous, and we used to cycle back starving to a huge greasy school breakfast and fall fast asleep right under the pulpit throughout the Sunday morning school sermon. Even after fishing, and deeply asleep in church, my thoughts seem to have been of Mick Jagger and Co., because on one memorable occasion I awoke violently in mid sermon and shouted out, 'I can't get no satisfaction! . . .' to the amazement of the boys around me and the giggling delight of the girls from the very posh young ladies' boarding school who always sat opposite us on Sundays. My Housemaster didn't seem to worry too long over what exactly was the deeper significance of Tarrant's dream. Tarrant was taken into the Housemaster's study straight after the service and given a damn good thrashing for being a disruptive influence.

SIX OF THE BEST

He was a great mystery to me, my Housemaster. I spent four years in his house and yet, although I seemed to meet him most days, I hardly ever saw his face. Usually I just got a message from one of the prefects telling me to go into the Housemaster's study, bend over and wait. After a long and uncomfortable wait I would hear his all too familiar footsteps coming along the corridor towards me, two large battered brown brogue shoes would come into my inverted eyeline, go past me to the base of a cupboard, open the door to take out something that made nasty swishing noises in mid air, then come and stop just behind me. Never a word was said, but there would be four, six, or, on one still hard to forget occasion, 12 red-hot burning sensations across my botty. Silently the brogues would go back to the cupboard, the door would shut and the shoes would walk away. If I met him today in the street I'm honestly not sure that I'd know his face, but I'd know his feet at once if he was still wearing the much-repaired brown brogues.

LOVE IN THE PLUM PATCH

The only girls we ever met at secondary school were the poor unfortunates who went to the Alice Otley school, a very strict boarding school for young ladies at the other end of town. They were kept under virtual house arrest the whole year round, wore white socks and had hairy legs until they were 18 and were caned in front of all the other young ladies if they were seen shamelessly holding hands with a member of the opposite gender. Needless to say these poor girls, cut off in the prime of their pubescence, were in the most rampant state if ever you could get close to one – but meetings were almost impossible to arrange.

There was a plum patch near the Alice Otley school and, if they could dodge the sweeping searchlights, barking dobermans and machine gun nests, it might be possible, with a lot of drainpipe shinning, to meet for a session of frantic heaving and thrashing under the plum trees. On Sunday mornings in church, which was the only time we were allowed officially within 100 miles of them, several of the young ladies always had unmistakeable plum stains on the backs of their light grey overcoats. The girls with plum stains became the most sought after by us boys. And they were constantly reprimanded by their terrifying, silver haired Headmistress for thinking lewd thoughts or showing a daring flash of whalebone body corset. Only later in life did I see the amusing point about this frightening old woman. It was her name: Miss Molest!

We spent most of our term time hatching incredibly complex schemes to get out of our dormitories into theirs, nearly all of which were disastrously unsuccessful. We wanted to be with the young ladies of Alice Otley, they clearly wanted to be with us. But always in between us were the barbed wire fence, the drain pipes, the dobermanns and, above all, Miss Molest.

In the holidays, though, we did meet lots of girls, sixties girls, who if they still didn't seem to want to come fishing at least would happily come round our houses and listen to Mick Jagger and the Kinks on the Dansette *Major*. They wore things like long white boots and mini skirts, but in the main, not having been kept under lock by Miss Molest for the past four years, didn't seem at all keen to hop into bed with steaming rampant schoolboys home for the holidays.

I have to report, sadly, that my love life in the sixties was a series of fiascoes. Fiascoes of young women suddenly sitting bolt upright when my hand reached the milky-white of their leg-tops and slapping me hard round the face. I spent my life pouring beer down seemingly very enthusiastic young ladies who would suddenly announce at three in the morning that they weren't going all the way on their first date. I was to learn through continued rejection that most of them didn't go all the way on their tenth date

either. I, like an enormous number of young men growing up in the swinging sixties, found that most girls weren't very swinging at all. The Pill of course changed the fear of unwanted pregnancy for a lot of women, but they were still very wary of boys' baser instincts, convinced that we weren't really interested in them as people, that we were 'only after one thing'. I have to admit shamefacedly that they were absolutely right.

THE SWINGING SIXTIES

I was one of millions of British males who missed out on most of this wild promiscuity that people kept assuring me was happening everywhere. Well, not in Reading it wasn't and not in Worcester, except in the plum patch. Come to think of it, when I went on to university in Birmingham there wasn't a fat lot of swinging going on there either. I remember thinking, 'Well we're all here, where the hell are the swinging sixties?' I have a feeling that four-fifths of the girls in England in the sixties were having sex with David Bailey and Terence Stamp and the rest of us blokes were getting virtually nothing.

I remember sitting for hour after hour in coffee bars making one cup of dreadful frothy *Espresso* coffee last seven hours and trying to phone a girl and losing all my shillings even though I'd definitely pressed button B. And coming out of three separate barbers on the same day with a fresh, ever shorter looking haircut, before I finally plucked up the courage to ask for a packet of johnnies please. And paying 3s 9d for three. And paying 4s 6d for one whole gallon of petrol. And spending most of the sixties preferring getting legless to getting laid . . .

Which was lucky since only Terence Stamp and David Bailey had the choice.

There wasn't an awful lot of swinging going on at Birmingham University in the sixties.

Off To School

Times Tables to Computers

OFF TO SCHOOL

TIMES TABLES TO COMPUTERS

All the mums and kids queued around this walled in playground. I didn't really know what was going on. I was togged up in new clothes and a satchel which had nothing in it. I thought this was great. I forgot all about my Mum. I remember looking around and seeing children howling and screaming. One boy, who later became leader of the local Hells Angels chapter, was sick with grief, wailing as if they had chopped his leg off. I couldn't understand all the fuss.

My first school was a funny little establishment for boys only in the middle of Reading. Like a lot of schools in those days, it was basically the Headmaster's house, a large rambling old building with very high ceilings and very dark rooms. The big heavy windows all seemed to have broken sashes and we were always being asked to open them, presumably to let the smell of us out, which invariably meant a risk of being beheaded as the huge windows came crashing down with no rope to stop them. I remember spending a lot of my early school life collecting broken glass.

The playground was the Headmaster's back garden, rubbed raw of grass by years of kids playing football on it. It was very hard and stony, and outdoor lessons like PE invariably led to a lot of badly cut knees, often requiring stitches. The equipment was all a bit Heath Robinson as well. I remember the vaulting horse being a tea chest that one of the Headmaster's family had brought back with all his kit in at the end of World War Two. It had a name, rank and number on it written in black paint, and another name, presumably the next of kin. If you didn't cut your knees on landing from the horse, you had every chance of picking up some quite vicious splinters on the way over.

The changing room and one of the classrooms were in a not particularly well-converted stable that still smelt unmistakeably of horse; and I clearly remember one of the goalposts at the end of our bone hard, rock-strewn football pitch also doubled as the frame for the Headmaster's wife's runner beans. We were asked to try to score most of our goals at the opposite end of the pitch.

The first Headmaster was replaced by a second who fitted very easily into the mould. He got all the bigger boys, mainly aged seven and upwards, to busy themselves for about three months building the school swimming pool. We took it in turns, each group missing a lesson a day, until the Great Construction was completed. I remember being particularly pleased because it meant on Mondays I missed Latin, and Thursdays I missed the incomprehensible algebra.

The pool was officially opened at the beginning of the winter term, an ideal time to start outdoor swimming in England. There was much trumpeting about our achievement in the *Berkshire Chronicle*, and the Headmaster was photographed a lot shaking hands with the Mayor, surrounded by carefully hand-picked children, mainly the ones who could manage the most sickening toady smiles. I was rather proud of *not* being chosen. What nobody from the *Berkshire Chronicle* seemed to have enquired was why the school pool was built without any sort of plan, and why it went from just over a foot at one end almost immediately to 18 feet about a yard from the edge, then back to a level four feet again all the way to the other side, except for a nine in sandbar right across the middle. Nor did anybody ask why it had been built right next to the Headmaster's wife's open plan chicken shed, so that the poor birds were regularly falling into the pool and being found dead the next morning. It also meant the survivors always left the water full of feathers and chicken droppings. Luckily it iced over quite early that winter, saving the lives of a lot of chickens and a lot of children.

With the Great Construction completed, I was volunteered onto a weekly rotor as Chlorine Monitor, which again was a very hit-and-miss affair. We used to pour the chlorine in from a huge earthenware pot and if you put your eyes anywhere near close it would burn your eyeballs badly. One day the Headmaster's idea of the exact amount of this deadly stuff to pour into the pool would be about three tablespoonfuls, the next day it would be a whole tin bathful. I suppose it depended on what the chickens had left overnight. He always used to tell us 'If it kills the frogs, it's just right for children to swim in.' Never mind the frogs, I think some mornings it would have killed a herd of buffaloes.

LATIN LOVERS

The other great drawback to the swimming pool being completed was that I was back to normal lessons, particularly Latin and algebra. What use the calculation of 'a' squared plus 'b' to the power of 'xyz' cubed was ever going to be to me I couldn't understand, and can't to this day. In my daily job as a breakfast Disc Jockey, I have to report that Latin hasn't been an enormous help. I think I first started doing *Amo, Amas, Amat* and *Hic Haec Hoc* when I was about six. Ten years later I just scraped through an O level and at last abandoned it forever. Never once since has the phrase 'Have you seen the spears of my brother, O Lentulus?' expecting the answer, 'Num plus the subjunctive' been a major conversation piece.

My Latin masters always seemed to be the Headmasters, as if only they could be trusted with anything so important. My first maths master, on the other hand, was unlikely to rise to a higher rung of the teaching ladder, mainly because he kept nodding off in class. He was very prone to violence, in fact he hit me hard round the head with his very knobbly fingers and/or the even knobblier wooden board rubber every day for about five years. Because he was very strict, even when he nodded off nobody dared to breathe, just in case he woke up and turned into Rocky Marciano again. I remember once he came in, hit me round the ear a couple of times just to be going on with, and then nodded off for the whole of the rest of double logarithms. When the bell rang for French after an hour and a quarter, we all tiptoed out leaving him happily snoozing away in front of the fire. He gave eight or ten of us a lift to school from time to time in his tiny old Vauxhall. It was a bit cramped but it saved us all our bus fares. It seemed a good idea at the time, and only now I realise that the paraffin stove he always had lit on the back seat because the Vauxhall's heater didn't work, was a bomb just waiting to go off.

Books, books and more books, spilling out of the school library — a world of make-believe that probably never existed. The untroubled worlds of Janet and John, Dick and Dora, the Secret Seven and the Famous Five.

School was tough. Most of the buildings were grim Victorian piles where generations of children had carved their inky initials in heavy oak desks. Uniform was compulsory and a clip round the ear was only one cheeky word away.

But rising in the bomb rubble of many cities were shiny new schools of glass and concrete — where Miss didn't seem quite so strict and you could always lure Sir away from the text of his boring lesson with 'Go on sir, tell us how you beat Hitler'. Chances were he'd tell you. . .

Mrs M Patterson of Liverpool recalls her pre-school days in the early fifties:

Piping hot steak and kidney and thick-skinned fluorescent blancmange beckons. Time to sprint the end of grace at 100 miles an hour: 'ForwhatweareabouttoreceivemaytheLordmakeustrulythankfulAMEN!'

I can remember from when I was about four and attending the nursery. In the afternoon all the children had to have a nap. There were rows of little canvas beds and whether you were sleepy or not you still had to lie on them. I can still recall the smell of the canvas and I laugh to myself when I think how carefully I would take my shoes off and arrange them so that I would not get them mixed up and put them on the wrong feet!

Classes were big — 40 or more kids was the norm. The three Rs (that's reading, writing and 'rithmetic) ruled, with *Janet and John* books in big type attempting to engage young minds and the chanting of times tables to bore them stupid. Still, there was always the nature table where catkins and dead beetles in matchboxes stood testimony to the wonders of the natural world.

Elaine Thomas of Nottinghamshire remembers the trauma of going to school for the first time:

Infant school days were traumatic. I hated being separated from my parents. My hair used to be tied in pig-tails, I wore kilts and pleated skirts which were held up with straps. Mum used to sew elastic onto my mittens and thread them through the sleeves of my coat, so as not to lose them. I remember the little liberty bodices with rubber buttons which kept out the cold. Every morning we would all sit cross-legged on the cold wooden parquet floor and sing hymns from the blue Songs of Praise *book. We used to get different coloured stars in our exercise books for good work. A gold one meant excellent.*

School dinners — ugh! 'Drink up your milk and eat your greens, all of them' — that was the message in a world just emerging from wartime rationing. 'Just think how lucky you are — people in India have nothing to eat. . . ' ('Well, they wouldn't want to eat this!')

All over the country at school dinnertime, mashed potato was dolloped out by grim dinner ladies wielding ice cream scoops — and a torrent of lumpy custard was ladled over a million roly-poly puddings. There was no choice — and always fish on Fridays. Free milk appeared each morning break time — and being milk monitor was a first taste of power.

Ann Harwood of Somerset first went to school in 1953 and has clear memories of that first day:

The first thing I remember was how tiny the toilets were. I thought they were for small people, not for a big five-year-old like me. And I'll never forget drinking my milk with a straw. We never had straws at home so this was quite a thrill. But then I got told off for bending mine and when I asked for another I was told there was only one each. I always ended up playing the bells or triangle in the orchestra when I really wanted to play the cymbals. And when it came to reading my Dick and Dora *books I always read "was" as "saw" and "saw" as "was".*

Out in the playground it was time to use our imaginations and invent games with rules so complex we'd forgotten them next day. Teams would form and disband, bonded together by magic passwords. And if you were caught a swift 'pax' (though you never knew what it meant) would protect you from some terrible punishment.

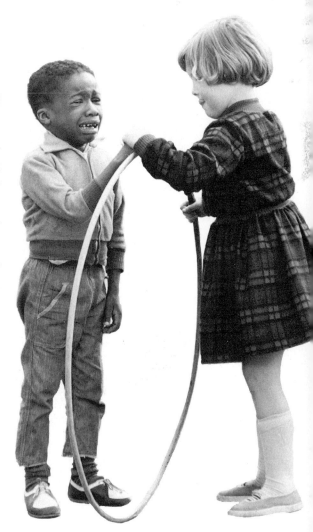

27

The big build-up and it's here: that First Day at School. Keep your chins up, chaps. Don't be cry-babies.

Mrs E Jarrom of Derby:

> *Talking in class was strictly forbidden. Anyone caught was made to stand in the corner until the teacher was satisfied that the culprit had learned their lesson.*

Corporal punishment at school was something you expected if you were naughty or didn't do as you were told. It was a whack with the cane, the strap or some other form of punishment either on the hand or rear-end. Cracks across the head were not uncommon for lesser misdemeanours. But such discipline guaranteed respect for teachers.

Greg Morrison of Staffordshire was regularly given the cane in his last years at junior school in 1958:

> *You didn't go home and tell your parents because they'd give you a good hiding as well and send you to bed or stop your pocket money. The kids of today don't know how lucky they are.*

. . . But school break was the best part of the day, as Jane Carr of London remembers:

> *The best playground games were on the slides we made when it snowed. We were fiercely territorial about them, and the right to go on a particular slide had everything to do with your place in the pecking order of friends and not-friends.*

Of course you weren't allowed to throw snowballs in the playground and there would be the watchful eye of Sir or Miss to make sure no such fun was had.

Margaret Woodhouse of Nottinghamshire didn't go to an inner city school, but she still came up against school discipline during those times:

> *I remember the freedom we enjoyed at school playtime during the early fifties. Being a small country school there were no railings and we were allowed to go out into the surrounding area, but if we weren't back when the bell was rung, we were punished by a whack on the hand with a ruler.*

A daily dose of calcium, an apple and some raw carrot — healthy elevenses.

School and schooling may have changed in the last 20-30 years but there remains that one common factor in all mixed schools. Boys think girls are 'orrible while girls think boys are smelly. Funny how we change our attitudes within a few short years.

Amanda Waters of Nottinghamshire fell victim to the boys' antics on numerous occasions:

I remember ink wells in desks at school and the pen nibs. Quite often the boys would flick ink pellets on rulers (when Teacher wasn't looking, of course). If caught, out came the cane for "six of the best".

Ink wells are no longer a school requisite; the biro and felt tip pen have seen to that. There is also no further need for mathematical tables now that pocket calculators make adding up so much easier (although many people from the fifties and sixties can still add up the 'old way' or divide by using the long division method more quickly than it takes the present generation to key figures into a calculator). And, of course, there were no computers at school in the fifties and sixties.

Yet more milk. The whole school day revolved around the arrival of crates of squat bottles of the stuff, frozen in winter, pushing the silver top up and out. Your turn to be milk monitor every time it was raining. And Mark Porter would spend a whole week shaking a bottle of milk to see if it turned to cheese.

And then there was Empire Day when traditional school rules seemed to be abandoned. In the late fifties Mrs Evelyn Fenn lived in Whitley Bay:

The boys and girls wore daisies wrapped in silver paper in their buttonholes. We girls wore ours upside down for some reason. The school piano had been trundled out into the infants' yard and our mums sat on wooden chairs and forms enjoying the performance. This year my class danced Strip the Willow. *The girls had been told to wear gaily-coloured dresses and ribbons in their hair – my dress was red and white with a pattern of strawberries. A team of boys from the top class put on a gymnastics display, thrilling us with their daring leaps over the horse. Everyone joined in the singing of patriotic songs to the accompaniment of the piano and this made us proud to be British. To hear* Rose of England *and* I Vow to Thee My Country *brings a lump to my throat to this day. Our childish enthusiasm waned somewhat while first the Head and then the Mayor made speeches. But we were granted a half-day's holiday to mark the occasion. How we cheered.*

But they were not all happy times. In the fifties and sixties hardly any homes had central heating and winter colds and 'flu were very common. In 1957 an outbreak of Asian 'flu claimed many lives, and inoculations against diseases like chickenpox and measles were only just being introduced.

Schoolchildren of the fifties could expect to be off school sick at least once a term – and when actually at school, this new generation of National Health Service kids could expect to be poked and prodded by an army of doctors, nurses and dentists keeping a watchful eye on their health.

Margaret Woodhouse, Nottinghamshire:

The dentist would come once a year with a caravan which would be parked outside the school for two to three days.

Parents made their own contribution towards keeping their children fit and healthy by dosing them with cod liver oil and *Haliborange* tablets.

Some mums got their babies on the 'health kick' at a very early age, as Elaine Thomas of Nottinghamshire recalls:

One horrible thing I recall is the awful, thick, brown, sticky substance that Mum kept in a jar on the top shelf of the pantry. It was called Virol. *I was given this daily, even as a baby.*

Just when you thought you were safe, after a childhood of jabs and stabs to protect you from a horde of malevolent illnesses, the doctors would come up with a new one. If you couldn't escape with the allergy excuse, you'd have to queue up for a public bravery test.

No matter what precautions parents and schools took against illness, many children were affected by polio, whooping cough and diphtheria and there were times when hospitalisation was necessary. Hospitals, like the schools, were often a throwback to Victorian days.

For a youngster, even something as simple as a tonsil operation, which was commonplace in the fifties, was a frightening experience, as Elaine Thomas recalls:

The next thing, they were placing a horrible black rubber mask over my face and I gasped for breath. On waking, it was dark in the room and my throat hurt so: I desperately needed to wee, but I was too frightened even to open my mouth, so there was nothing for it but to wet the bed.

NEW CONCEPTIONS

And sex was beginning to rear its head. By the mid sixties it was on the telly and all over books and magazines so it was impossible to keep at least talking about it out of the classroom.

Sex education began in biology lessons, where nervous sirs and misses, having explained to their class how snails reproduce, at last got round to the mysteries of human reproduction — with big illustrations on the blackboard to make it all perfectly clear.

Chances were the class knew quite a lot already . . . 'Stop sniggering at the back!'

At the age of eleven, schoolchildren faced their first big obstacle race — the Eleven Plus exam which would divide them into the rougher, tougher secondary modern lot and the smarties who would go to grammar school.

It was an unfair system and the Eleven Plus exam was gradually dropped, the idea being that everyone, including late developers, should have at least a second chance.

The new concept was the 'comprehensive', modelled on the American high school where children of all abilities could go. The first comprehensive was opened in Kidbrooke, south-east London, in 1954.

The political rows were stormy as old-established schools were shunted together into big institutions. Sometimes these had thousands of pupils, but supporters of the comprehensive idea could point to the big science laboratories and sports facilities that having lots of pupils allowed them to build.

Jim Finn of Liverpool made the transition to senior school in the early fifties:

I was born in 1942 and life was fairly predictable. County primary school first, where pupils were placed in one of two streams. The upper stream prepared pupils for the Eleven Plus exam for entry into the grammar, technical or commercial schools, and the lower stream was for those who just went along for the ride unless they showed some academic promise, in which case they were transferred to the upper stream. Most pupils wore blazers and short grey trousers while the posher ones would have a school badge stitched to their blazer pocket.

So much for lessons — with the new mixed comprehensives a girl had more important things on her mind.

Comprehensive schools were mostly co-educational and thus brought an end to many single-sex schools. The arrival of the comprehensives also coincided with a new prosperity in Britain, and children found themselves going on school holidays to places like Italy and France or skiing in Austria – something their parents would never have dreamt about.

Inevitable changes occurred and one age-old tradition, daily morning assembly, has since ended in many schools. In some schools it is now held just once or twice a week, and is often split amongst different year groups, on account of the large number of pupils involved.

The change of school entailed subjects never before encountered at junior school: woodwork, metalwork, chemistry, physics, French, Latin and so on, as pupils were educated to a standard good enough to sit the GCE examination which replaced the School Certificate in 1948. In 1951 headmasters criticised the new examination, stating it was too hard for many students, just as they criticised the GCSE 25 years later.

In 1961 the Government launched its new 43-letter phonetic alphabet. It was tried as an experiment on a thousand primary and infant schools, but was scrapped in the seventies.

Mrs E Fenn of Whitley Bay remembers moving schools:

In September 1960 I became a pupil at Tynemouth High School. Feeling strange and uncomfortable in my new uniform I waited in the girls' yard with two friends from junior school, until we were rounded up by a prefect. It was easy to spot the first-formers, as we were all wearing too-large blazers and had berets on our heads. The first-year boys, over in the other yard, were just as conspicuous in their short trousers and school caps. We soon learned that hardly anyone bothered with a beret or cap after the first week!

We were taken through this vast building and told we would know our way around after the first week. There were so many different classrooms, we found this almost impossible to believe, but it was true.

New subjects like French and science were on the curriculum. "Lessons" became "periods" and "playtime" became "recess". Worst of all, there was a homework timetable, with two or even three subjects every night.

For a timid 11-year-old, it was all too much to bear. After my first day I cried myself to sleep.

School uniforms played an important part of the strict schooling in those days; it was a sign of disciplined times. But uniforms were often costly items and could only be purchased from specialist outfitters who charged in excess of the normal price of a blazer. Many mothers felt that in the case of their daughters this was an unnecessary expense because they would be leaving school at 15.

PE: the school gym was a haven for some and a hell-hole for others. Music and movement. Pretending to be a tree. Making the fat boy do the vault over and over again. Strange apparatus that would swing out from the walls to form an adventure playground of climbing and hanging upside down. And at the end of term, if you were lucky, a game of pirates for everybody to enjoy.

The schooldays of Mrs J Davey of Bristol were 1953-63 and she remembers her school uniforms:

In 1953 I started senior school. I remember the big fuss of shopping for school uniform which consisted of gymslip, white blouse, tie, blazer and gaberdine raincoat – the normal requirements for an all-girls school at that time. After two years the gymslip could be substituted for a wrap-around skirt. I also remember the shoes and socks: brown lace-ups and long fawn socks in winter and leather Clarks sandals (always the same two styles) and white ankle socks in summer. Then of course there was the school hat: velour in winter and a panama in summer; heaven help you if a prefect caught you with it off in a public place.

School days were certainly memorable times. They were happy times, they were frustrating times. But whether they were the so-called 'happiest days' of one's life remains another matter.

Tricia Reed of Brixton recalls:

Outside your new bungalow school buildings, you could stand in line and twirl the latest American import as part of official school training. Before things got heavy around Eleven Plus time, there was plenty of fun to be had at school: glazing pottery, making Christmas doilies, hitting xylophones. It would never be that easy again.

Around 1958 I failed my Eleven Plus examination and was sent to a secondary modern school in Stockwell, about two miles away, which involved a bus ride and a long walk. My lasting impression of those days was of taking three hours to get to school because of the smog. This black smelly mess came down into the atmosphere regularly, creating what was known as a "real pea souper". The air was acrid and you were advised by your teachers and parents to cover your mouths at this time. Some of us overdid this a bit and were unable to breathe properly until we got to school. Our clothing and hair must have smelt awful.

Every November, just after the Harvest Festival, the jockeying for position in the Nativity Stakes began. The star roles of Joseph and Mary always went to someone else. Third shepherd was a poor substitute, even with a tea-towel round your head and a battered crook for disguise.

Auditions for school plays were always a trial, but it was the nativity which brought the devil out in us. Parents competed for the best costume and the rustle of crêpe paper and tinsel could be heard almost before Harvest Festival was over.

Sarah Rainford lived in Cumberland in the sixties and remembers the good times in school at Christmas:

Christmas at school was probably the same across the whole country. We all dressed up in our little angel costumes, with halo and wings made out of coathangers bent into shape and outlined with tinsel. Being of fair stock I coveted the role of Mary (Why did Mary always have to have long dark hair, whilst blonde locks only qualified for the ranks of the hoard of angels?)

LIFE AT HOME

MOD CONS AND SELF SERVICE

LIFE AT HOME

MOD CONS AND SELF SERVICE

When Mum wasn't cleaning the house she was cleaning us. She was always washing and ironing. Dad's suits and shirts had to be immaculate each morning for work. And I had to go off looking like little Lord Fauntleroy. My father seemed more-or-less contented with having his life organised for him like that. He worked hard and he didn't want to think about whether or not he had clean pants and socks. He always did of course, just in case he got run over . . .

I remember my fifth birthday party, if only because it was the first and last time that Timmy Davis came. At the time he seemed just a nice friend that I used to play with, but on reflection I think he was probably quite mad. His main contribution to my party was nicking three jellies, putting them all on top of his curly head, and combing them in neatly with my Dad's comb — pinched from out of the bathroom. From then on it was all downhill. Pin the Tail on the Donkey turned nasty because he pinned the tail on David Dodwell instead, drawing blood and causing him to scream in pain. And at the end of the party, when it was time to say thank you for having me, Timmy was nowhere to be found. He eventually turned up about 300 yards down the road on the slate roof of a pub and was brought down by a fireman on a long ladder, his hair still covered in nicely combed red jelly . . . He's almost certainly a Cabinet Minister by now.

Mum always seemed to be working. Although she didn't go out to work I don't think I ever once saw her sitting down. She was fanatical about keeping the house clean and neat and tidy. She was constantly scrubbing and polishing. The kitchen always smelled of *Lifebuoy* toilet soap. Dad and I lived in fear and trembling of making marks or coming in with muddy footprints. Given a few spare seconds she'd have polished the coal.

We lived in constant fear of diseases. Mum gave us ghastly things like cod liver oil and the disgusting *Virol* to keep colds away, a vile pair of forerunners to the modern vitamin pills, but there were still all sorts of nasty things that we kids knew we could catch, many of which have now pretty much disappeared. I remember Mum taking me to the doctor for a series of recurring backaches, and being asked, 'Is there much TB in your family?' This of course made me much more alarmed about my visit to the doctor than I already was. Mercifully my backache turned out not to be Tuberculosis, but growing pains caused by shooting from five foot three in to six foot two in a single year. Diphtheria was still a threat to young children, as was whooping cough. At school we were constantly being examined for ringworm and having our partings inspected by the nit nurse. Nits were quite a problem, there were two or three outbreaks at our school. There was always a certain amount of social stigma attached to the poor luckless families that had got nits among them, and the children had to go home with plastic bags on their heads, which made the whole thing even more degrading. But it was the luck of the draw who caught the nasty little things.

The great fear was polio, which crippled and killed hundreds of children in the fifties. Hot summers seemed particularly likely to produce a polio epidemic. I remember the great shock when a Bishop died of the disease after visiting some polio patients in hospital. I lived in constant fear of catching it. I remember sitting on trolley buses, knowing all the statistics, and working out how many of the people on the bus would catch polio before the summer was over. Hopefully I got my maths wrong. Today the fear has been taken away with a sugar lump, but in my childhood it was a shadow over us all.

THE DREADED DRILL

Dentistry was a bit basic as well. Luckily I never really needed to go to the dentist until well into my teens, by which time things had got a bit more hi-tech. Till then my only dental problems had been wobbly milk teeth coming out, after which I'd find sixpence left under my pillow by the tooth fairy. However, I did have to go to the dentist to hold my Mum's hand. There was an old wicker basket that they threw extracted teeth into, presumably to be emptied annually — all very hygienic. Any fillings were done by an incredibly slow, and presumably incredibly painful, hand drill. From the grim details I still remember it's little wonder I didn't go anywhere near a dentist's surgery till more than ten years later.

Mum and Dad seemed incredibly happy. There didn't seem to be any real rows or threat of imminent divorce and none of their friends seemed to talk about divorce either. The man went to work, the woman stayed at home, they lived together and had children and made the best of it. We were vaguely aware of people having affairs, but only really people in the newspapers. There was the Duchess of Argyll scandal, where polaroid pictures were accepted as evidence in court for the first time. The pictures were of prominent people's privates — apparently some of the privates were pretty damned prominent as well. Not really understanding the word 'privates', I read the story in the *News Chronicle* and wondered why there was so much fuss about a lot of photographs of young soldiers. There was Norma Levy with her strange collection of whips, manacles

and masks, and later the Profumo affair shook the establishment. But in the main my Mum and Dad's generation seemed content with their lot and got on with their lives together for better or for worse. It was our generation that wouldn't settle for that, and divorce became as much a part of our lives as the Pill.

Dad worked hard to keep us all ticking over. He was very proud when we finally had enough money to buy our first house. It was a small semi-detached about 30 miles from London on the Old Bath Road. It cost the frightening sum of £2,000. We lived there happily enough, Dad working all day but usually getting home in time for dinner in the evenings (made on our new GEC electric cooker), and saving hard for his first car, a Wolseley 1500.

Home was where the heart was. In the fifties at least. Mum would be found in the kitchen baking a cake, and Dad in the parlour listening to Antony Eden on the wireless. But the new prosperity, that was bringing motor cars and foreign travel within reach of ordinary families, was beginning to transform home life. Washing machines, hoovers and convenience foods gave women a new kind of freedom, while — most significant of all — a big brown box with a small black and white screen was set to invade every living room. The age of television had arrived and home life would never be the same again.

But not everybody had the luxury of electricity, as Margaret Woodhouse of Worksop recalls:

The thing I remember most vividly about the fifties is the day I arrived home to find we had electricity. Having been used to oil lamps, candles and a primus stove, which was used to heat the kettle, it was so exciting to simply flick a switch.

Families were trying to get back to normal and with men home from service there came the biggest population boom in Britain since 1880. By the end of 1959 there were four million single people between the ages of 18 and 25.

It's hard to believe today that Britain was bankrupt after the war and rationing went on until 1954 when we joyfully burnt ration cards to celebrate the occasion. There were even identity cards until 1952.

The 1951 census revealed an increase in the UK population of 3.8 million in 20 years and ten years later this had increased by a further 2.5 million, including 353,000 immigrants. To meet the demands of the population growth a record 347,605 new homes were built in 1955. However, despite full employment in Britain in 1957, 2,000 people per week were reported to be emigrating to Commonwealth countries.

Brothers, schoolfriends, the boy nextdoor. By 1963 over two million British lads had done their National Service. For some it was the time of their lives, for the rest a nightmare.

Back-to-backs cultivated a whole society lost to the tower-block madness of the seventies. As Alan Sillitoe's Arthur Seaton said in Saturday Night and Sunday Morning, 'Don't let the bastards grind yer down.'

Sleep sweeter-
Bourn-vita

Made by Cadburys

This was the heyday of tea and collecting cards infused with tea aroma and sticking them into albums. We'd swap them to make a full set but always end up with six copies of the RNLI lifeboat. And with tea we had Mum's home-made biscuits and Dundee cake.

Jim Finn spent the fifties in Liverpool:

> *Fathers worked long hours all week, including Saturday mornings, while mothers stayed at home to look after the house, bake and sew. Life was very much a matter of strict and standardised routines. Money was in short supply and people lived in back-to-back terraced houses in narrow streets. There were real street communities. The main mode of transport was the tram. Coal, bread, and milk were delivered by horse and cart.*

All babies born in the fifties were National Health babies, courtesy of Aneurin Bevan who introduced the service in 1948. And many were brought up according to the teachings of Dr Spock in his famous *The Common Sense Book of Baby and Child Care* which was launched in the United States in 1946 and went on to sell 25 million copies worldwide.

Maureen Ramsey also lived in Liverpool in the fifties:

> *I was the eldest of five children and Saturday night was bath night, starting with the youngest. Our hair was combed with the "biddy" comb before it was washed. Our clean clothes were all laid out for Sunday. Galoshes or pumps were whitened with Blanco, a small block of whitening. Our teeth were cleaned with Gibbs toothpaste which was in a solid pink block and came in a little round tin. Woe betide anyone who dropped the toothpaste and broke it!*
>
> *On a Saturday evening at 6 p.m. a van would draw up outside the house and my Mum, who was waiting eagerly, could hire a little Hoover washing machine for half a crown. She had it ready by 8 a.m. the next morning when it was picked up. Everything we could lay hands on was washed — cushion covers, curtains, etc.*

Rinso was one of the most popular washing powders in the fifties — its advertisements used to boast: 'Used by more women than any other soap powder in the world'.

But it was not only the house that Mum wanted to clean — it was also the kids, as Mrs S Thomas of Bridgend remembers only too well:

Every morning there was a spoonful of cod liver oil before we went to school, and once a week syrup of figs ("To keep your bowels open", I can hear my Mum say!)

We hated every Saturday night 'cos it was bath night with added Dettol *which, if we had cuts, would sting; but it was nice afterwards to get into clean bedsheets. A lot of people who didn't have a bath could pay for one at the public baths by us. My best friend who lived in the Peabody Estate, top of Lambeth Walk, she had no bath — only an old tin one put in front of the fire. We were lucky.*

Every Monday was Mum's turn for wash day; tenants took turns once a week. She spent all day in the communal wash house amongst the steam and boilers. We couldn't afford a washing machine. We didn't have a carpet either, just a square runner in the middle of the living room, the rest of the flat was lino.

Every Monday we had to have rock salmon and chips from the chip shop.

Suddenly everything was bright, clean and probably plastic. And 'advertising' had suddenly arrived. It was chic to wash with Rinso **and mangles were strictly manual.**

To have bought a Hoover washing machine in the early fifties would have set you back £25 plus £6 tax. It was the equivalent of approximately six weeks' wages. Other modern-day necessities like the telephone and fridge were unheard of and in 1950 only 46 per cent of British households had a bathroom. Outside lavatories were commonplace.

Amanda Waters of Nottinghamshire remembers those not-so-far away days when luxuries were a thing you only dreamt about:

Our house at the time had an outside "bucket" toilet, a pump in the yard for water, and no bathroom. When it came to bath night, out came the tin bath. The coal fire was stocked up, and slowly water heated by the panful for a warm soak in front of the fire. The lights were gas.

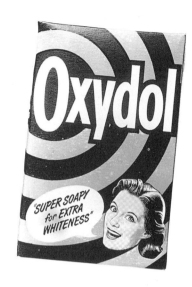

Forget those wash-day blues, put on that Hardy Amies dress and step up with father's sweaty socks . . . lucky me! Automatically the best! After all a girl owes it to herself.

Mrs M Patterson, Liverpool (fifties):

"The house we lived in, like many of the houses around us, was very run down in the aftermath of the war. A lot of homes still had gas mantles, but we were lucky enough to have electricity. We never knew what it was like to have hot water coming out of a tap though. There was an outside toilet and our bath was a tin one which was regularly hauled in and filled in front of a big coal fire.

I came from a large family and my mother was forever scrubbing and cleaning. Sometimes I wonder why she never gave up – it was like flogging a dead horse. My Mum and Dad must have been so tired looking after all of us but I never heard them complain. Many a time if Mum or Dad had made a big pan of scouse, our friends were invited to stay and eat with us. Many of the families in our street were in the same position as ourselves and the feeling of closeness from that community still remains with me.

We also had our fair share of vermin. We were that used to it that it was nothing to see rats and mice running past us, and some of those rats were as big as cats. Sometimes it would be so bad at night that sleep was impossible. Often at night myself and my older brother, who was four years older than me, would wait until everyone was asleep and creep downstairs. We could not step into the living room right away, the reason being that when the light was switched on all the cockroaches would scatter everywhere. Once we were in the living room we would rake the remains of the coal fire and fill a tin with sugar and margarine. It would then be placed on the hot ashes and, as we thought then, be turned into toffee. It was like eating a brick and I am surprised that I still have my own teeth."

What a luxury! A self-service launderette. For 2s and 6d you could wash a 9lb bundle, expose your smalls to the neighbours, watch the soap bubble all over the floor and gossip to your heart's content.

Tony Grantham from Greenwich, London, revelled in a man's world:

> Little boys wanted to be real men. It was either engineering or sport. Tinkering with Dad's car engine and rebuilding bikes. Trains (the real thing or the Hornby models), Mamod, Meccano, gliders made from balsa wood. And we dreamt of clean-cut centre forwards and rubbing linseed oil into tough leather boots. As for the new Action Men — wot, dolls for boys?

THE HAPPY SHOPPER

Other well known common household goods and their prices in 1950 were: *Beechams Powders*, two for 5½d (2p), Robertson's *Golliberry Jam* 1s 5½d (7p) per pound, *Germolene* 1s 6d (7p), *Kolynos* toothpaste 1s 3d (6p), *Daily Mirror* 1d (less than 1p), *Marmite* 2s (10p) for 2oz, Seven Seas cod liver oil 1s 6d (7p), *Embassy* cigarettes 3s 6d (17p) for 20.

A mass observation pilot study of 700 working class homes in the London area in 1951 revealed that most women did their shopping on Fridays and spent between 10s (50p) and £2. In 1957 the average food bill was £1 8s 1d (£1.40) per week.

In the early fifties, luxury items like an Astral fridge would cost you £37 9s 8d (£37.49), a Hoover *375* cleaner would cost 15 guineas (£15.75) plus £3 18s 9d (£3.94) tax, and a leather cloth three piece suite would cost £27 7s (£27.35) or 5s 9d (28p) per week.

By 1969 the bank rate had risen from two to eight per cent since 1950 but so too had average wages (to £24 16s 5d – £24.82 – per week). Some prices in 1969 were:

Tefal non-stick milk pan £2 2s 6d (£2.07), 20 *Guards* cigarettes 4s 10d (24p) for 20 with coupons, a top quality brand chicken 2s 6d (12p) per pound, *Daily Mirror* 5d (2p) and *Golden Meadow* butter 2s 3d (11p). And some electrical items: a Ronson hairdrier £3 19s 6d (£3.97), Bush record player 23½ guineas (£24.67), Philips three speed food mixer £7 19s 6d (£7.97).

Shopping in the early fifties was very much as it had always been – a trip to the grocer, the baker and the butcher to buy the staples of life. Mum could have a gossip over the bacon counter while up and down the land, in the tiled emporia that had survived from the Victorian age, money would be whisked away on a mysterious overhead railway – to a place at the back of a shop where a fierce old lady with her hair in a bun would hoard all those threepenny bits and half crowns.

But the new age of the wire basket was dawning. In 1950 an old established grocers called Sainsburys introduced a 'self-service' store in Croydon. A year later Premier opened something they called a 'supermarket' in London's Earls Court.

Mrs Jarrom of Derby remembers shopping in the sixties:

When I was a small child supermarkets as we know them now did not exist. Instead, Mother used to take us shopping at the Co-operative Society. The entrance was very grand with two heavy wooden doors graced by brass handles. Inside was an oversized grocer's shop with goods stacked high on cumbersome shelves which totally covered one wall. The counter seemed to go on forever and was so high I could barely see over the top.

Mother would produce a list from her purse and read out each item required to the attentive shop assistant, who would collect the items with some reverence from the shelves and place them on the counter in front of Mother.

After all the items on the list had been gathered together, Mother would ask how much the bill came to; it was usually around £4. A £5 note would be handed over and we children then directed our gaze towards the ceiling. Up there stretched several sets of wires, all leading to a little office high above us.

Mother's £5 note and the bill were loaded into a small carriage attached to the wires. With a quick twang the carriage was propelled like a miniature cable car towards the office. Once there, both bill and money were removed and the change and receipt propelled back to the waiting assistant. By this time the groceries had been packed into Mother's shopping bag. All this happened at a leisurely pace, most unlike the push and shove experienced in modern supermarkets.

Identity cards were abolished in 1952, but in the aftermath of the war, rationing remained in force until 3rd July 1954. Meat was the last item to be regulated and when all rationing came to an end there was a mass burning of ration books to celebrate the occasion.

For a country girl like Mary Bitcon of Cumberland shopping was an excursion in the early sixties:

Life outside the village extended as far as a mile away to the nearest shop. Our own tiny village shop resided in my elder cousin's front room (parlour) where her family stocked the basic tinned foods, sweets and stamps.

The trip to the big shop always took place on a Thursday. My mother, grandmother, aunties and others, with children in tow, would gather by the village green mid morning. Once all were assembled the journey would commence on foot, regardless of the weather. There was always a battle between my sister and myself as to who would push the pram of one of the younger members of the flock and who would lead the dog, or at worst have to carry a shopping bag.

On reaching our destination each of the women would take it in turns to gather their supplies for the coming week whilst the others waited by the door catching up on local gossip; there wasn't room for everyone inside the shop!

The supplies were neatly wrapped, packed, tied up with string and labelled to be sent on to the various addresses by van later that afternoon. Only then would the slow walk home begin.

Fresh vegetables and fruit would arrive on a Tuesday by horse and cart. Whilst the grown-ups were weighing the potatoes we would sneak an apple or two to feed the horse.

All produce would be grown locally. Potatoes, sprouts, turnips, tomatoes, onions etc. There were none of the exotic fruit and vegetables which are available today. Avocado pears were unheard of! Even mushrooms on toast were considered a sheer luxury, the ultimate treat!

Friday was the children's favourite day. The day the "pop" man came. You had a choice of three: lemonade, orangeade or Dandelion and Burdock. *The pop man also brought the crisps. These were purchased by the box and kept in the bureau in the parlour, and guarded ferociously by my father along with the* Dandelion and Burdock.

If we behaved when we went out to play, we could look forward to a bottle of pop, sickly cream soda, **Dandelion and Burdock** *or fizzy* **Tizer** *— don't spit in the bottle!*

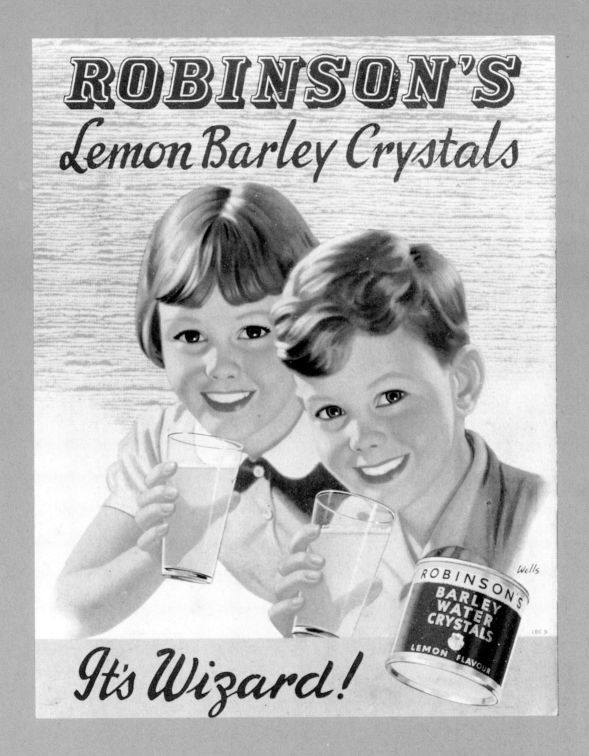

Advertisers suddenly realised that it wasn't adults who governed how much was spent and on what, but children. As Miss Brodie said, 'Give me a girl at an impressionable age, and she is mine for life.'

"I love my new English Electric Refrigerator"

Obviously she knows what's what when it comes to choosing a refrigerator. This gleaming beauty is the ENGLISH ELECTRIC EA-83—and there's enough room inside to take a banquet. Even the door is a larder !

Lots of refrigerated storage space means lots of advantages. You can do a week's food shopping in a day. You can plan your meals well ahead. Left-overs won't 'go off'. Cake mixes and vegetables can be prepared to-day and stored until needed. Here is the refrigerator to give you a fresh interest in food, more fun and more leisure. And remember, it only occupies just over 5 square feet of floor space—fits any moderate sized kitchen comfortably !

TO READ AND THINK ABOUT

More than 15 sq. ft. of adjustable shelf area—giant, full-width Freezer—special Coldrawer for meat and fish—two big Humidrawers for fruit and vegetables— and three generous shelves in the door itself! White or cream enamelled finish.

ON PARADE NOW

See the ENGLISH ELECTRIC EA-83 at your local ENGLISH ELECTRIC Authorised Dealer or Electricity Service Centre. Hire Purchase terms are available. Cash price £100.12.0. Purchase Tax extra.

ENGLISH ELECTRIC

BRINGING YOU BETTER LIVING

The ENGLISH ELECTRIC Company Limited, Domestic Appliance and Television Division, East Lancashire Road, Liverpool 10

CLEAN CRAZY

Keeping the house clean was a pleasure — well almost — with hoovers for the floors, washing machines to handle the clothes and a host of other labour-saving devices. The weekly shop came in as the larder went out, with new efficient refrigerators enabling the housewife to store food for longer periods. The influx of bits and bobs was never ending — but with little money to spare and no credit cards they had to be budgeted for.

Everybody was saving up for something, as James Hughes, from Hackney, London recalls:

There were months of preparation when we were going to get something new for the house. Lots of planning went into the purchase of a three piece suite, or some new item like a fridge or a TV. You didn't just pop down to Argos and stick it on a card! It was a major event.

It was the age of the labour-saving device. Everything was electric and everything was for sale. For the first time you could buy your kitchen gadgets door-to-door. HP was the thing, credit did not just appear in the eighties.

Probably none of us had a mother who wanted to set her own hair and cook at the same time but it was possible, and that was the main thing. Utility furniture was the height of chic from the flop-down sideboard and the ubiquitous stool to hairdrier and mixer. If you could afford it, you would buy it. Homes were packed to bursting with the new designs.

In the mid fifties before telly began to rule the home, the wireless had a last golden age. The news on the Home Service was still read out in sombre tones by men in dinner jackets and bow ties and you certainly wouldn't hear Elvis Presley or Bill Haley on the 'Light Programme', but there was a new mood in the air and on the airwaves.

The first 'Goon Show', broadcast at the beginning of the fifties, was completely anarchic and weird in contrast to the staider radio comedies of the time like 'Take it From Here', or 'Much Binding in the Marsh'. Meanwhile, Grace Archer was famously killed in a barn fire while Mrs Dale confided her thoughts to the nation in 'Mrs Dale's Diary'.

There was one place where you might hear a 'pop' record. Uncle Mac, the presenter of 'Children's Favourites', might quite suddenly play *You Ain't Nothing But a Hound Dog* to break up the tedium of the *Run Away Train* and a *Four Legged Friend*.

Bob Reed of Dartford regularly journeyed into space through the fantasy world of the wireless in the fifties:

Home entertainment was centred around the old valve radio, where the highlight of the week was "Journey into Space" with Jet Morgan, or, on the constantly fading Radio Luxembourg, "The Adventures of Dan Dare".

My first experience of music must have been at the age of three, with a pre-war wind-up gramophone. It only played 78s and the needles had to be changed regularly. The sound came from a cupboard into which I could crawl, close the doors and blast myself with various classical recordings and the old forties standards — the only records in the house.

Colour television was still many years away but you could buy a red, green and blue transparent plastic sheet to stick on the screen and give it a coloured tint. And for those small 12-in screens you could buy a magnifier to screw to the front of the TV set.

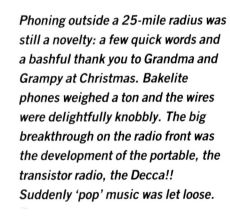

Phoning outside a 25-mile radius was still a novelty: a few quick words and a bashful thank you to Grandma and Grampy at Christmas. Bakelite phones weighed a ton and the wires were delightfully knobbly. The big breakthrough on the radio front was the development of the portable, the transistor radio, the Decca!! Suddenly 'pop' music was let loose.

As the sixties arrived and televisions started to invade most living rooms, Sunday was still the one day for listening to the radio, as Geoff Cousins of London remembers clearly:

At midday "Two Way Family Favourites" brought requests from the British forces abroad to the folks back home: "Looking forward to seeing my granddaughter for the first time in September on her third birthday." It all seemed terribly sad.

Then, with the windows streaming with condensation and the inevitable roast on the table, a primeval scream would issue from the wireless: "Wakey Waaaaaakey!". "The Billy Cotton Band Show" accompanied the main course but it was the pudding that was the high point of the day. That combination of apple crumble, custard and Jimmy Clitheroe has yet to be beaten.

With Mum safely back in the kitchen and Dad prostrate on the sofa (these were the days before women's liberation, you must understand) it was time for "Movie-Go-Round", a bizarre concept in that it attempted to preview feature films on the radio.

The next couple of hours remain a blur although they generally involved the construction of elaborate helicopters and speed boats from clothes horses and sheets.

The voice of Alan "Hi There Pop Pickers" Freeman dragged us back to the wireless at five o'clock. For the next two hours he skilfully worked us up into a frenzy of anticipation. Who would be number one? The Beatles or the Stones? No one else seemed to get a look in.

Leaving us on a high, "Fluff" vacated the airwaves condemning us to the audio equivalent of a bottle of Mogadon. I'm talking of course about "Sing Something Simple". The mere mention of the Mike Samms Singers still sends me into a deep depression.

The big day in the life of many families in the late fifties was the arrival of the television set. Telly had been around since before the war but only for the richest families — and before commercial television began in 1954, the BBC's output was stuffy and middle class.

Mrs J Davey, Bristol (1953-63):

I attended the local junior school and came home in time to listen to "Mrs Dale's Diary" and "Children's Hour". We spent a lot of time listening to the wireless. The year was 1953. That year I saw television for the first time — we crowded into a family friend's home to watch the Coronation. After this many families started to have television sets. We got one the following year. I remember it was a monstrous thing with double doors over the screen but transmission was only for a few hours in the evening so I still listened to the radio a lot and read lots of books.

I recall being constantly bored and, as an only child, spending a lot of time with adults or escaping into the world of make-believe.

On Sundays the whole family would settle down to watch TV. Early TVs were as solid as a chest of drawers. And children's TV, when it came, was equally sensible: Muffin the Mule clip-clopping on top of Annette Mills' piano.

Mrs P J Gerrish of Bristol recalls that memorable day when the TV set arrived:

My Dad said we'd have one if I passed the Eleven Plus: "It will help you at grammar school." But the Cup Final was on the weekend before the results of the exam were announced so we got one anyway (so much for helping at grammar school). It was 1953 and the Coronation was due on June 2nd, so we were suddenly very popular.

We only had a small bungalow, and the set was in a small dining room. In one corner went the table, and all the chairs were marshalled into position. Some people even brought their own. Old friends, neighbours and even the bachelor curate all squeezed in, and put their lunch offerings on the table in the corner.

The grown ups "oohed" and "aahed", while the kids got progressively hungrier. Nobody could feed us until the crowning was over. Even then, the women were concerned with making sure the curate had everything he wanted before we were let near the goodies . . . and we had to say Grace.

Then commercial telly roared in with bold and brassy game shows like 'Take Your Pick', and 'Double Your Money'. The BBC fought back with shows like 'Crackerjack', 'Hancock' and, on 23rd November 1963, Dr Who began his Saturday tea-time travels.

Not to have a television was a terrible fate, like being cast into outer darkness, when playground games revolved around the 'Adventures of Robin Hood' ('It's your turn to be the Sheriff!') or 'Rawhide'.

Because of the hire purchase boom, a television set was to be found in most British homes by the sixties. In 1960 itself 10.5 million television licences were issued and the average viewer sat in front of the screen a mere 12 hours per week. By the end of the sixties that figure had increased by 50 per cent and included nearly 100,000 colour licences. Colour television, introduced in 1967, was the biggest step forward since the launch of BBC 2 in 1964 and the appearance of television's first advert (for Gibbs *SR* toothpaste) on 22nd September 1955.

. . . and what can you say about Helen Hill's (Merseyside) selections?

My favourite television programmes were: "Andy Pandy", "Merry Go Round", "Mary, Mungo and Midge", "Sooty and Sweep", "Trumpton", "Camberwick Green" and Disney films.

Mick Ord of Liverpool remembers some of those great productions of the sixties:

I remember "Torchie the Battery Boy", "Larry the Lamb", the first episode of "Dr Who" and Barry McQueen. Barry who? – A BBC newsreader who one day in 1964 told the watching millions he was returning to his homeland, Australia. (Wow!)

TV was a novelty for my Mum and Dad, and the tiny Pye, BBC-only set was seldom switched off. I never knew what it was like without a set, which is why I thought my Grandad was crazy trying to interest me in a top and whip set, especially as I was missing "Fireball XL5". Television increasingly became the source of my perceived wisdom, creating domestic drama where hitherto there had been calm waters.

Children's TV was short and sweet – 15 minutes of "Watch with Mother" and the "holy hour" between five and six o'clock. "The Woodentops" and "Rag, Tag and Bobtail" were my favourites. "Bill and Ben" were endured. Mainly it was adult TV that provided stimulation. "Tuesday Rendezvous" and "Abracadabra" are as much a part of my consciousness as Steve Zodiac and Tonto. "The Fugitive" was the stuff of nightmares (not for me of course, I being a boy and in the Cubs, you understand, but for my younger sister). The one-armed man appeared so often in her dreams that in the end the heavy hand of the maternal censor intervened.

Being a Dalek was the prime playground aim in the early sixties. The cry of 'I-AM-A-DA-LEK!' became the chant of millions of schoolboys — and girls. For the more sensitive there was 'Andy Pandy' — what did he get up to with Teddy in that basket? — 'Bill and Ben' and Little Weed, and later 'Camberwick Green'.

Sunday was always a special day and the one day of the week that was looked forward to. It seemed to be so different to the other six days of the week.

Barbara Theaker of Halewood also has fond memories of Sundays in the fifties. She was the eldest of a family of nine girls and boys:

Each Sunday, weather permitting, the oldest of us girls had to take the little ones to the local park. Our picnic would be one penny's worth of "fades" (bruised fruit – we could cut the bad parts away) and a bottle of water to which we'd add lemonade crystals. In the evening after tea and the obligatory sing-song around the piano or listening to the old wireless – "Journey Into Space" and "Take Your Pick" – we would bring in the tin bath, fill it with hot water and, two at a time, would bathe in front of the fire (sometimes made up of old shoes and lino when there was no coal!)

Margaret Stafford of Gateshead also has her views on the reason why she was sent to Sunday school:

Sunday school played a big part in our lives in the early fifties. My sister and I used to attend Duncan Street Mission, off Sunderland Road in Gateshead. I was in the Rechabites, although I wasn't sure what that was, and still don't know to this day. The building was tiny (it is still there, used as a store) and a congregation of 30 was a crowd! We always went to Seaburn for the outings and were solemnly handed our train tickets and a shilling's spending money before we all walked along to Felling Station.

Gradually, my friends began "defecting" to Moore Street Chapel. Each year we "moved up" and the big ones had their Sunday school in the pews of the church. During Anniversary week, we sang hymns in the surrounding street, accompanied by a portable organ, and collected money for chapel funds. I hated doing it and thought it was begging.

There were things that television did not replace – Sunday school – as Geoff Cousins of London recalls (sixties):

Nothing transports me back more readily to a Sunday morning in the early sixties than the smell of over-boiled sprouts.

The day would begin with the enforced trudge to Sunday school; a ritual that owed more to my mother's need for an hour of peace than any desire on her part that I become a man of the cloth.

The journey back included the inevitable detour to the sweet shop: a Jamboree Bag (with liquorice laces and a flying saucer) or a Barrett's Sherbert Fountain in winter. An Ice Pop in summer. Maybe even some Spangles. (Whatever happened to Spangles?)

ON THE ROAD

However, days out were few and far between. They were often long and tedious affairs since very few families owned a motor car. But as families became more prosperous, thanks to near full employment and the fact that 25 per cent of all Britain's married women went to work by 1959, there was a new-found affluence. Luxury items were now within the reach of many families (thanks to hire purchase in a lot of cases).

A new Austin A40 cost £685 in 1951. There was only one model, unlike today when you can choose between 30 models of the same car. A Ford Popular in 1953 cost £390 and in 1969 a Mini would have cost £595 10s (£595.50). For those who could afford it, the open top version of the 'E' Type Jaguar, launched in 1961, cost £2,097 15s 10d (£2,097.79).

The 1950 Budget put 9d on petrol tax which took the price to around 3s (15p) per gallon. Five years later it was up 50 per cent to 4s 6d (22p) per gallon.

The thrill of the first family car is recalled by Mrs Jarrom of Derby:

Until I was about eight years old, we always walked everywhere or took the bus, but then in 1964 my Dad decided it was time we became a car owning family.

For weeks we were filled with excitement and anticipation. Finally the day arrived. There on the drive stood one black Ford Popular, the latest thing on four wheels. We all piled in, Dad and Mum in the front, my brother and I in the back. We felt like royalty cruising down the road at 30 miles an hour!

It only had three gears, plus reverse, of course, and was available in just one colour – black. The windscreen wipers were most peculiar: the faster the car was travelling, the slower the wipers would go. If we were caught out in a shower we would have to slow down to see out of the window.

The acquisition of a new car was a major event. Dad came home proud as punch and the children would pile in for a spin round the block. A new A40 was something to boast about.

Out To Play

HOP SCOTCH TO ROBOTS

OUT TO PLAY

HOP SCOTCH TO ROBOTS

We played for hours in the streets around our home, in the park and in a great open space near the main railway line to Paddington. For a few years before I went off to boarding school I was a fanatical train spotter. A gang of us used to go down to the railway line near Twyford, race round and round a sort of scramble course on our bikes, but leap off at the approach of any train, grab Ian Allan's Bumper Book of Trainspotting *and underline the train's number as it raced past.*

As an only child I spent an awful lot of my time playing by myself. When I got older I spent an awful lot of time playing with myself . . . but that's neither here nor there. Because my school always seemed to go on holiday last, and then stay on holiday last, most of my mates were back at school while I was hanging around the house bored stiff. Occasionally when I was a bit older I'd make the effort to go into town for the day but it usually meant hours of hanging around a coffee bar trying to make one coffee last forever without getting thrown out.

A lot of the time at home I would play all alone and talk to myself. My mother was constantly calling out 'Chris, who's in there?' and I'd feel thoroughly embarrassed and say, 'Nobody Mum, it's just me talking to me again.' I'd have games of football with a balloon in our lounge and I'd award a penalty against myself for tripping myself up and then, just as suddenly, I'd be the England goalkeeper and save the penalty that I'd awarded against the other team in the first place. I'd play cricket with a plastic ball full of holes, and I'd always score at least two centuries before lunch and then open the bowling for England and take all ten of the Australians' wickets before tea, only to rattle off another high-speed 100 before close of play. The sort of conversation that my mother would overhear would be me as the batsman arguing with me as the umpire as to whether I was out or not. Invariably I wasn't.

When my little gang's holidays did all coincide we were quite a force to be reckoned with. We all used to go to a very evangelical free church on the outskirts of Reading, where we were constantly being asked to 'Let me hear you say "Yeah!"' and 'Offer your souls to Jesus'. It was all terribly serious at the time, and at the age of eight most of us made the Big Decision to give our lives over to the Lord. Inevitably by the age of nine we'd forgotten all about it and were if anything more revolting and ungodly than we'd been at seven. But the church was very much a meeting place. Most of us joined the Cubs, 'Dib dib dib, dob dob dob', and then went into the Scouts until we just got too embarrassed to go round in silly khaki shorts any longer.

SCOUTING AROUND

The Cubs and Scouts period was a truly great time of my life. It got me into the country a lot, which I loved, and camping holidays were something we looked forward to all year. Mum and Dad would somehow come up with the princely sum of £1 10s, and we would be off in the bus, with free board and lodging under canvas for a fortnight. We played Scout games, we told our first dirty jokes, we learnt our first dirty songs, and we swore every morning to be clean in thought, word and deed as we Scout-saluted the Union Jack.

We had one very strange Scoutmaster who insisted on us all exercising naked every morning and wrestling nude after lunch. We thought this perfectly reasonable at the time, it was something to do with the air getting more easily to our young bodies. Years later he was arrested.

I must have spent four years in the road outside the Cub hut. We played football of course, usually with a tin can, and we played obscure games like 'tip cat' that nobody ever really understood, but I usually won because I was the accepted authority on the rules, most of which I invented on a day-to-day basis. This skill presumably came from years of cheating against myself when playing alone.

We hung around the streets and then when it got dark, but before it was time to go indoors, we moved our bikes a few yards and sat under a lamp post. We always took our bikes, but must have spent two or three hours a day sitting on the saddles, feet on the ground, going absolutely nowhere. Once in a while we would all rush home to whoever's house had a television in it, almost certainly black and white, to watch something really unmissable: 'Quartermass and the Pit' was one. But, even though it was beginning to gain quite a foothold in the world of the grown ups, television meant very little to kids in the mid fifties. Nowadays we have non-stop 'Home and Away' and 'Neighbours', and I think on balance I'd rather be sitting under a lamp post on my blue bike.

Most of our machines were painted garish colours and had things like cow handle bars and fixed wheels. My Dad, who'd also been a mad cyclist when he was young, would tell us proudly of the day he'd been cycling at high speed on a fixed wheel down the very steep hill into High Wycombe and was suddenly overtaken by his front wheel. My bikes were rather safer than his, but in any case we were expressly forbidden to use the main roads. Although traffic by modern standards was virtually non-existent, there was no speed limit, no breathalyser, and it only took one careless Zephyr Six, Sunbeam Rapier, Morris Traveller or Ford Popular to flatten a little boy on a blue bicycle.

Sadly exactly this happened to one of our gang. One night as we cycled home from a fishing trip, we spotted flashing lights, an ambulance and the remains of what was unmistakeably Keith's bike on the main A4. There was a lot of blood for a long way up the hill and at the top of it the crumpled body of our friend. Apparently he had a dynamo light on his bike that used to work on the principle that the power is being provided to the light all the time you are pedalling. Poor Keith was stationary in the middle of the road, waiting to get across, and of course not pedalling. The car that overtook a Mini simply never saw him. Keith died without ever seeing the sixties. CT

Playtime in the fifties often meant kicking a football round a bomb site. Santa didn't have much in his sack; perhaps a chemistry set, a Dinky toy, or, if you were a really posh kid, a Hornby Dublo train set.

Then the toymakers discovered plastic — perfect for Making anything a child could desire: dolls and *Action Men*, a *Scalextric* motor racing track, a 1:72 scale construction kit of the *Bismarck*.

And plastic was just right for making throw-away toys, which suddenly everyone seemed desperate to have, and just as suddenly were out of fashion in later decades. There were lots of them — hula-hoops, yo-yos, Scooby Doos, clacker balls . . .

Mrs M Theaker of Liverpool:

We used our imaginations to invent games, like kick-the-can and a kind of high jump. The mothers would come out and play rounders in the street with the children.

Maureen Ramsay also lived in Liverpool in the fifties and remembers how she used to have fun:

My earliest memories of the fifties are of the evenings in the winter, calling at our friends' houses and enquiring; "Any swaps?" We would sit on the stairs, a gang of us in the cold, swapping comics for hours on end. On Friday afternoon after school we would visit our grans, aunts or neighbours for any empty pop bottles, beer bottles, etc. In fact, anything with a 2d return on the bottle for our money for the pictures the next day. Maybe we would be lucky and have enough for a Mickey pop lolly, 1d faded apple, or a bag of broken lolly ices from the corner shop as well. We would run errands and do anything to make a little extra money.

Summer afternoons were spent feeding the ducks in the park and playing top and whip (the top was from a lemonade bottle and the whip a piece of wood with string tied on). If we had some water and lemonade powder and jam or egg butties, we thought it was great. They were happy times.

Make-do-and-mend was part of every boy's motto. A go-kart was a status symbol. Nick a couple of pairs of pram wheels, an orange box, a broom and your Dad's old coat, and suddenly you were Donald Campbell . . . so long as the engine had enough puff.

But there were still reminders of those not-so-long-ago war days, as Bob Reed recalls:

At the back of our estate were the remains of a Canadian gun emplacement complete with a jeep left over from the Second World War. Milk crates and corrugated iron littered the place and we would use these to build camps. Dartford received a few German bombs during the war and there was quite a lot of shrapnell strewn across the countryside which we kids used to collect.

One day an entire unexploded incendiary bomb was found by one of the older boys. My mates and I found out that he had hidden it in the old air-raid shelter at the bottom of the garden, so we relieved him of it! We were happily throwing the bomb around in my garden when the old chap nextdoor came home from work and nearly had a heart attack when he saw us. Next thing we knew, the police had taken charge of it. Just as well because it was still full of explosives even though the detonator was faulty.

Pram and pushchair wheels were prize finds on dumps and bomb sites as these, together with three pieces of 4 in × 4 in timber, an orange box, a few nails, nuts and bolts, and a length of rope, could easily be constructed into what we called a trolley. The two large pram wheels went at the back with the pushchair wheels at the front. One kid would steer while the other would sit at the back and propel it with his feet.

Greg Morrison of Staffordshire remembers his football playing days in the street:

Of course there weren't the cars on the road as there are today. We used a tree as one goal post and the lamp post as the other. The number of times I scored the winning goal for Wolves in the Cup Final or for England in the World Cup is countless.

If we were rained off it was into somebody's house to finish the game either with Newfooty *or* Subbuteo *teams.*

For children growing up in the fifties and sixties, going out to play meant just that, and it was in the street that gangs were formed, games were played and friendships made and broken.

Boys always played football in winter and cricket in the summer. Girls had their own games, as Elaine Thomas of Nottinghamshire remembers:

There were seasons for different games: the whip and top came out at Easter, together with marbles and hopscotch. Summer saw the usual rounders, cricket and skipping with Mum's clothes line. We used to make a tent in the garden by covering Mum's large wooden clothes horse with blankets.

Behind the allotments or over the 'rec', we'd find a few pop bottles and get the deposit back down the corner shop. After splitting the money, we'd flick tops — winner take all.

Jim Presswood from Yorkshire recalls the camaraderie on his road:

Being poor and only having hand-me-down toys didn't matter so much. The street was there as a huge adventure playground itself. If someone had a bike, it was the street bike, and everyone could ride it.

85

Vince Rutterford lived in Edmonton in the early-to-mid sixties and remembers those great days spent playing in the street:

The most vivid memory I have of being a child in the sixties is of the street as the social centre of the world. Every human drama would be carried out there. Now the street has simply become a place to walk or, to be more accurate, drive through.

Looking back, the streets were always free of traffic; the roads and pavements were one big playground. Of a summer evening there'd be groups skipping . . .

I like coffee,
I like tea,
I like Susan in with me . . .

and bike races, cissy girls, piggy boys and home-made scooters. At seven-thirty Mum would shout us home for bed and we'd moan and moan and moan until washed, tooth-brushed and pyjama'd.

Nar, nar, I'll tell your Mum you've been lying on the ground!

TOYS FOR BOYS — AND GIRLS

Train sets were the most cherished of all boys' toys while girls spent hours playing with their dolls' houses and prams in the fifties. Dolls, of course, were baby dolls in the pre-*Barbie* and *Sindy* days. It was not until the start of the sixties that dolls which looked like fashionable women became popular with young girls.

Boys also had constructional toys like Airfix models and *Meccano*, and, of course, there were the ever-popular Dinky cars and lead soldiers which are now worth a small fortune. There were none of the remote-controlled cars or electronic games of today. The nearest to eighties' silicon-chip technology was the *Magic Robot* quiz game.

A TYPICAL SATURDAY IN THE FIFTIES

8.30 a.m: Breakfast consumed, togged up in pale green V-necked jumper, grim-coloured "white" shirt, black shorts and brown brogues. A quick glance out of the window to see who was out. It was then off into the street with Mother's cry of "Don't get dirty, or else . . ." ringing in the ears. The balsa wood airplane with its wings shattered at one end and held together by two strips of Sellotape *would be retrieved from its hiding place under the hedge. In fact every hedge had its own hiding place, which was known to all the kids of the street, where stores of marbles, elastic bands and golf balls were kept. Anyone was allowed to use them, just so long as they were put back in their original place.*

Washing going up on the lines and idle chit-chat; it was the same every Saturday morning. We'd be tearing up and down the street, hiding in the gardens and going through the throes of death countless times whilst playing cowboys and Indians.

At the end of the road there was a pub, complete with off-licence, and when you entered there was usually no one there because they were serving in the bar. To stop thieves, there was nothing on the counter except a jar of arrowroot biscuits — the equivalent of caviar to us kids. The difficult part was that a bell announced your entrance to the shop, so you hoped that they were busy serving otherwise they'd be at the counter in seconds. If they arrived too soon, you would have to buy ha'pence worth of Black Jacks *or* Frutellas *instead of getting the "free" arrowroot biscuits. On top of costing you money there was the added injury of looking wet in front of your friends. No matter how many biscuits you got from the jar it was never enough to satisfy your gang's pride — somebody had always taken more.*

After a few hours of shouting, kicking cans, grazing knees and other tom-foolery, as if by magic mothers would appear at their doors to recall their offspring, spruce 'em up and drag them off shopping. Saturday's freedom would come to an abrupt end.

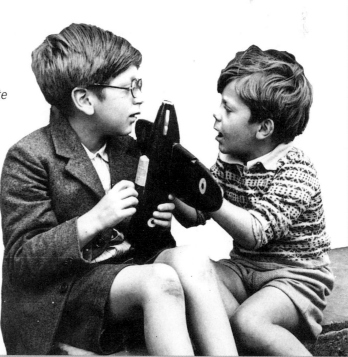

Every tree had a rope slung from an upper branch by an older brother or father. And every rope had a boy or tomboy hanging from it vying for who would swing the highest, or do the hardest dare.

90

Helen Severn of Nottinghamshire remembers:

Summer days and evenings at the local "rec" where we spent hours polishing the slide with waxed bread paper and a candle to make it really slippery.

Adventure playgrounds, which became commonplace in the sixties, were actually introduced in the fifties and the first ones opened in Peckham and Notting Hill Gate in 1951.

Local parks were places of great fun where you had the choice of unvandalised swings, slides and roundabouts. All sorts of ball games were played and a park keeper made sure things didn't get out of hand.

Mrs P J Gerrish of Bristol recalls those happy days:

We tied our skipping rope (and a small boy on one occasion) to the lamp post in the middle of the road, dropping it reluctantly if a lorry came by. All the skipping rhymes which we thought were new, but of course weren't, were part of our games. There were rituals for "dipping", for "sardines" or hide 'n' seek: "One potato, two potato, three potato four . . . and out goes she". We banged two old tennis balls against our garage (no car, just a garage) door, to the fury of my mother. We stood on our hands, dresses tucked in knickers, and kicked the paintwork with our feet.

Some lucky few of us had roller skates, but you couldn't skate on the road because the gravel tickled your feet, so you had to risk the wrath of any childless avenue-dweller by doing "arabesques" along the footpath.

The boys occasionally broke a window with their football, but they usually adjourned to the local playing field. We girls weren't allowed over there often because of nasty men. We chalked hopscotches, snail-like, oblong, and two-one patterns, on the road and paths. If there was no chalk, we'd find a good piece of oolite stone — it worked just as well. Factions formed and re-formed over the ownership of those hopscotches, and you were cruelly mocked if your parents were first to call you in at dusk.

Then suddenly, we all became 11 and 12, and senior school put its tentacles around us. Now we'd hang about the avenue, sitting on walls and talking, sizing up the boys we'd once played with. Street games were strictly for kids.

And the summers were always hot and the countryside not far away. Mum and Dad would pack a picnic during the holidays and we would tag along across the fields to a spot by a stream. And we'd have Marmite sandwiches, peanut butter and banana, salmon fish paste, or sandwich spread, all on thick, white bread from Homepride. On the way home we'd fall out, Dad would get angry and one of us would howl with grief as the sun sank low and the street lamps lit.

Frank Smith of Cheshire:

After being told off by neighbours for playing football in front of their houses, we would return later and either knock on the door and run away or tie two door knockers (no doorbells then) together, pull the string and run away. It was fun watching them both struggling to open the door, until the string broke.

Joe Marshall, Cumberland (sixties):

Coming from a close-knit community, about the only risqué act we got up to was tapping the local phone box (the old style "press button A", "press button B"). We would devote whole evenings to harassing our friends or the operator with comments like, "Get off the line, there's a train coming!"

February 27th 1958. The new toy craze is the pogo stick, mastered here by the nine-year-old Taylor quads of North London. When not at school they practise their skills fearlessly bouncing along the road. Watch out in front, here we come!

Christmas 1953 and a Hornby Dublo railway attracts children of all ages at Bentalls store in Kingston. We all know what these lads would like in their Christmas stocking!

And then what about some Dinky toys from Gran and 'Meccano, the Toy of the Century! — Nothing gives boys greater pleasure than finding out what makes the wheels go round . . . Meccano is just the toy for them.' Unless, of course, you were a potato head!

Everyone had Fuzzy Felt and anyone who was anyone had a Golly. Paper Gollies were hidden behind Robertson's jam jar labels and we were all mad about collecting them.

The fashion-conscious tot of the fifties and sixties would go out in frills, making sure 'baby' was safely in her cot. Going to the shops, of course, required a pram — latest model — and a wholly different outfit.

Jenny Durber from Hampstead in London:

My brother and I used to sneak into the local toy shop. It was stuffed with toys of every kind from floor to ceiling and an old man — he must have been in his forties — stood behind a counter. He looked over and down at us as I hunted out a Fuzzy Felt for, I think, 1s 3d. My mother kept it; it's upstairs now.

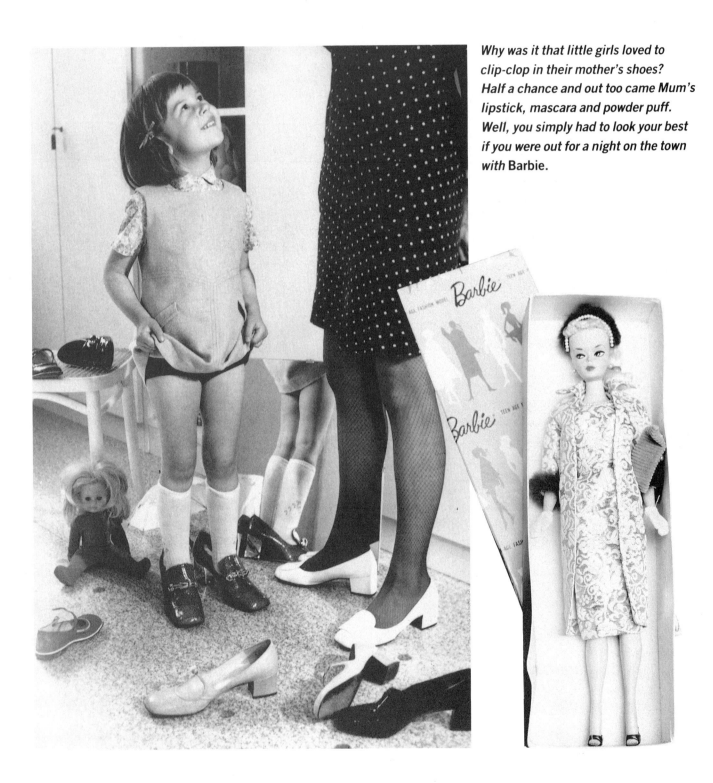

Why was it that little girls loved to clip-clop in their mother's shoes? Half a chance and out too came Mum's lipstick, mascara and powder puff. Well, you simply had to look your best if you were out for a night on the town with Barbie.

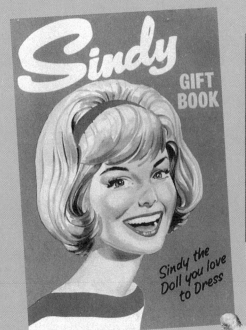

Sindy
GIFT
BOOK

Sindy the Doll you love to Dress

OFFICIAL
EMERGENCY
WARD 10
NURSES UNIFORM
AS SHEWN ON TELEVISION

BY PERMISSION OF TELEVISION PRODUCTS LTD.

A career for a girl was confined to being a secretary or, of course, a nurse, as glamourised by 'Emergency Ward 10'. In any event you would eventually become a housewife, so why not practise on this fully fitted kitchen?

MORE
RUPERT
ADVENTURES

But Barbie *was not the only chick in town.* Sindy *arrived and girls everywhere wondered what a blonde bombshell was. But if life became too racy you could always escape with trusty old Rupert.*

And for boys, with the 'Cold War' at its height the only thing to do was take up arms and drill till you dropped . . . well until Mum called you in for tea. In Dundee the lads couldn't afford guns so they pillaged the waste-paper bins for missiles to throw at one another.

Boys liked playing with guns and made up their own war games. They were also mindful that they would one day be called up to serve their country because National Service, introduced in 1939, was still compulsory for all 18-year-olds, who were required to serve two years. The last men were recruited on 17th November 1960.

Bob Reed certainly lived dangerously:

We were crazy about all forms of home-made weaponry. Mum's metal nailfile, the best dinner knives, Dad's putty knife and any other suitable items would regularly go missing only to turn up later, converted into a spear or arrow head. We would hoard penny bangers from Guy Fawkes' night throughout the year, and then during the summer holidays various features of the local terrain would disappear in a loud, unexpected explosion. The more adventurous kids would buy weedkiller, mix it with sugar and pack it into tubes. This practice soon stopped when one boy on the estate blew his hand off in the garden nextdoor. I had busted up with him only days before. I still think of him – it could have been me.

We were always on the look out for catapult "prongs". Any ideally shaped branch of a tree plus very powerful ¼ in square section elastic that could be obtained from the local cycle shop would do the trick. Our catapults were always being confiscated by the police, as were our sheath knives. I still don't know to this day what the real purpose of that ¼ in elastic was.

Dan Dare, Pilot of the Future, flies to investigate the nine moons of Saturn. Dan's space ship is seized by the traitor Blasco who, aided by Saturn's rulers, plans to become Emperor of the Earth . . . Lucky we had our Dan Dare Ray Guns close to hand.

Sales of space toys rocketed after the first moon touch-down. You joined forces with your friends' toys and pioneered that first landing over and over again.

Amazing what sweet cigars did for your image . . . Or there was the ultimate party prize — a bumper pack.

The Cubs and Scouts, Brownies and Guides. In 1960 there were thousands in Baden Powell's fraternity. Why was it you always got the prize for doing the stupidest thing at camp?

UNIFORM LIFE STYLES

The Cubs and Brownies were stepping stones for the Boy Scouts and Girl Guides and the days out to the seaside, parks or local zoos were looked forward to with eager anticipation each year.

Trips out were the ultimate of treats because people didn't have cars.

The Boys' Brigade, Army Cadets and so on were stepping stones for eventual conscription as Jim Finn, who grew up in Liverpool in the fifties, recalls:

On a Friday night the kids were allowed to attend the Life Boys (a junior Boys' Brigade) which involved wearing a sailor's hat and navy blue jersey, doing drill and playing games. Conscription was still in force then and many youths gravitated towards such uniform organisations.

Cinema audiences in the fifties and early sixties remained large as the likes of Flash Gordon and Roy Rogers came to the silver screen. People still laughed at Laurel and Hardy and Charlie Chaplin. They fought every battle with John Wayne and revelled in the brilliance of such actors and actresses as Richard Burton, Liz Taylor, Cary Grant, William Holden, Vivien Leigh and Grace Kelly.

Jim Finn had dozens of cinemas to chose from for his Saturday afternoon matinée in Liverpool in the fifties:

> *Saturday afternoons you would be allowed to go to the matinée at the local picture house to see such all time greats as* Roy Rogers *and* Hopalong Cassidy *at a cost of 6d, with 3d for 2oz of sherbert lemons.*

In 1962 a post-war record 126 films were made in the United Kingdom. Four years later this figure was down to 69, the lowest total since 1947. Television played a significant role in the demise of the cinema and many picture houses were turned into tenpin bowling alleys as the new game from across the Atlantic became the fastest growing participant sport in Britain. But, by the end of the sixties, it too suffered the same fate as the cinema and bowling alleys became bingo halls. (In recent times there has been an upsurge in cinema popularity and tenpin bowling is also making a comeback.)

'We are the minors . . .' The Minors' Matinée on Saturday morning: for a few pence you could be thrilled by Roy Rogers and Zorro, laugh along with Laurel and Hardy and stuff yourself stupid with a pennyworth of toffee. Who cared if your older brother or sister went out that evening to see 'proper' films?

"WEST SIDE STORY" ROBERT WISE PRODUCTION STARRING NATALIE WOOD

RICHARD BEYMER · RUSS TAMBLYN · RITA MORENO · GEORGE CHAKIRIS

DIRECTED BY ROBERT WISE AND JEROME ROBBINS · SCREENPLAY BY ERNEST LEHMAN

CHOREOGRAPHY BY JEROME ROBBINS · MUSIC BY LEONARD BERNSTEIN · LYRICS BY STEPHEN SONDHEIM

BASED UPON THE CONCEPTION OF JEROME ROBBINS

BOOK BY ARTHUR LAURENTS · ASSOCIATE PRODUCER AND CHOREOGRAPHED BY JEROME ROBBINS

WEST SIDE STORY

Cinerama, *which added a new dimension to movie-watching, made its début in 1952 and the following year saw the launch of CinemaScope. And it was after the launch of the new technology that such epics as* Ben Hur, West Side Story *and* Lawrence of Arabia *graced the screen.*

Stratford Hotel in the year 1749

"SAFETY CURTAIN"

Bob Reed took time off from weapon-making and devilment occasionally to go to the cinema:

The highlight of any week for a kid in the fifties was the Saturday morning pictures. After being led in song by the manager (We are the Grenadiers or something like that) before the show, we would then cheer on our heroes: Flash Gordon, Captain Marvel, and Hopalong Cassidy. We were very territorial about where we sat each week and any kid sitting in your seat was asking for trouble. A pomegranate or bag of peanuts afterwards completed the morning.

So popular were the Saturday morning pictures that a comic called Rocket *came onto the market, featuring all the characters we were watching at the cinema. It was a very glossy affair, on a par with the* Eagle, *but sadly it disappeared after only a few issues and nobody else I have met since can recall it. Comics regularly gave away free gifts but the one that for some reason everyone seems to remember is the* Whiz Bang *given away with the* Beezer. *It was, after all, only a triangle of card folded in half with a folded triangle of brown paper inside, but it would make a loud bang when you whipped it downwards.*

Other popular comics of the day were the *Tiger* complete with Roy of the Rovers, who eventually branched out and got his own weekly comic. The girls were treated to the *Bunty* and the *Girl* while, of course, Desperate Dan, Korky the Cat and the likes, were still entertaining us in the *Beano* and *Dandy*.

The comics were the best thing: Beano, Dandy, Wizard, Topper, Victor and all the others. If you were a girly swot you might even pick up a book or two when the gang wasn't watching.

School holidays were that six week period which seemed to last forever, reflects Mrs S Thomas of Bridgend:

During the school hols it was swimming or collecting old newspapers and empty bottles for money. The rag man would put bundles on scales and give us money, but we used to put bricks inside to increase the weight.

Mrs P J Gerrish of Bristol was one of the few who went away every year. But even she did not appreciate how lucky she was:

Every summer we migrated, like the swallows, from the southern heights of Bath back to my parents' home town in Kent. The other kids in the avenue thought we were the luckiest pair alive. Five whole weeks at the seaside; it was unheard of in the early fifties. Typically, we were ungrateful. "Can't we ever go anywhere except Sheerness?" we moaned.

Looking back, it was the excitement of our year. Leaving school on the last afternoon and rushing home, being collected by taxi, yes, a taxi, and whisked off down to Bath Spa station. Then it was a quick dash up the dozens of stairs onto the platform, up to the far end, and an impatient dance until the steam engine rushed by, and we hid our eyes and ears in fright.

London came slowly. The special treat comics were exchanged and read, and by Box Tunnel we thought we must be nearly there. Disillusioned, we immediately demanded food and drink, which we consumed all the way to the first sighting of the Thames near Reading. Then we finally bustled into Paddington.

Now came the big decision, taxi or underground. If it was a taxi we'd see Buckingham Palace, but Mum insisted on the underground. Dad and I were away, cases and bags flying, down the escalator. Poor Mum had the unenviable task of luring my younger sister onto the moving horror, while Dad stood at the bottom yelling "Hurry up, the train's in!"

Soon came Victoria, and the hunt for the electric train to the Kent coast. We rocked and crawled through the orchards and hop fields, until we all tumbled out into the dark at Sittingbourne. Across the platform and into an old chugger to Sheerness-on-Sea. Too dark to see whether the tide was crossing the Swale, but oh the joy of the lighted buckets swinging from Ridham Dock to Kemsley's paper mill. At last, the lights of the big wheel at Sheerness fun fair.

Summer hols were so eagerly awaited that you nearly burst with excitement when the day came. The romance of Great Yarmouth, the intrigue of Clacton, the sheer extravagance of Brighton or Bournemouth . . .

HOME AND ABROAD

Holidaying at home in 1950 was usually either in a guest house or Holiday Camp. A week at Atherfield Holiday Camp on the Isle of Wight would have cost £5 5s (£5.25) whereas a week at the Walton House Private Hotel in Clevedon was between 5 and 7 guineas (£5 5s and £7 7s). In 1959 Pontins advertised fully inclusive holidays from £10 per person per week, or for £15 you could rent one of their chalets, inclusive of fridge and television.

Mrs Janet Gill of Leicester remembers her first experience of holiday camp life:

In 1962, when I was only five, my first holiday camp holiday was to Warner's at Corton near Great Yarmouth. I remember mealtimes with silver service waitresses and nappies tied round the chalet door knobs to say whether you had a sleeping baby inside.

I also remember gaining independence as I got older when we went on these holidays. To borrow any of the sports equipment etc. you used to have to hand in your chalet key against the loan of these and my parents always asked for a spare key for my own personal use.

By 1960, 3.5 million Britons were holidaying abroad. By the end of the decade the 'package' holiday had certainly arrived and holidays in Majorca cost as little as £28 17s (£28.85) per week. Twenty years earlier the cost of 16 days in Spain was £68 but in 1957 you could get bed and breakfast in one of Spain's newest resorts, Benidorm, for 110 pesetas a head. That was the equivalent of 19s (95p) per night. Britain's first air charter holiday company, Horizon, started operating in 1950.

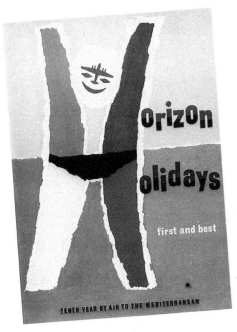

And if you went to Butlin's well, weren't you the one. 'Morning campers!' Two weeks of going beserk, running your parents ragged, cheeking the Redcoats – 'cos they couldn't answer back – and every evening so exhausted you could hardly flop into bed before you were fast asleep.

HAVE A *Wall's*

GOOD AND BIG!

It's nice when you're out and
It's nice at home too.

So why not take home some Wall's
at 1/6d or in Tubs at 6d ?
from the Wall's range

Going away on a week or fortnight's holiday was the annual
excursion for the chosen few. For others it was merely a
day at *Blackpool* or *Margate*.

113

As new prosperity meant more motor cars, the sooty smell of a journey by steam train was replaced by the sticky vinyl of the back seat of Mum and Dad's Ford Cortina.

But the steam age was ending anyway. The last steam engine, named *Evening Star*, was built in 1967, and four years earlier Dr Beeching had announced the cuts in British Railways that would sweep away rural branch lines and close 2,000 stations.

Trainspotting, along with stamp collecting, were the two most popular hobbies for boys, and Richard Thomson of Birkenhead remembers those great days of the steam train in the fifties:

When I was young all boys wanted to be train drivers and I was no exception. From my earliest days I was spellbound by the sight, sound and smell of those massive steam trains thundering up and down the country. I was taking engine numbers before I could properly read or write.

My local station was Birkenhead Woodside, where I used to join other train spotters in the hope of "copping" another GW 2-6-2 tank, a Stanier 2-6-0 or LMS Class 3 tank. The day that the driver of LMS tank 40110 asked me on the footplate I was in euphoria. As pocket money allowed, I used to travel to Chester where the cream of motive power would be seen — Great Western "Castles",

"Granges" and "Halls" and LMS "Patriots" and "Royal Scots", I remember to this day the sight of 5008 Raglan Castle — copper-capped chimney and safety valves (furiously blowing off) and brass nameplate and, of course, the lined-out green livery at the head of a train just arrived from Paddington.

My father was a commercial traveller and I often used to go out for the day with him. One favourite railway location where we often stopped was near Leyland, Lancashire, on the West Coast main line. We timed our stop to see the down Royal Scot and this produced the ultimate of "cops" — a Duchess Pacific, often in maroon livery. With its crimson and cream livery, the speeding train provided a truly impressive sight.

Again, as pocket money allowed, I used to go on "shed bashing" trips — organised coach trips by railway enthusiast societies. Walking up and down rows of steam engines, some in steam, some cold, often on a frosty day in winter, was an experience never to be forgotten.

Now aged 45, I am still very much a railway enthusiast. I often yearn for the trains of the fifties — the steam, oil, sulphur (remember the smell of the carriage seats?), the dirt, the colour and the deafening noise — fantastic.

Incidentally, I never did become an engine driver.

It was fun to be a train spotter when trains were alive with steam and smoke and sparks. You needed the requisite notepad and pen, but no anorak as yet . . .

All the fun of the fair. Whirling for twopence on the Merry-Go-Round with Mum while Dad was left holding the goldfish. Too much excitement, though, and there'd be tears before bedtime.

Fairs have always been special places of fun and it was there that most people enjoyed their first candy floss or 9d hot dog, came off the Waltzer feeling sick but pretending they enjoyed every minute of it, and experienced their first ride on the Big Dipper.

At least Sarah Rainford of Cumberland admits that some of the rides were too scary for her:

One of the highlights of the year was the annual funfair at the nearby town. Compared to today, what a small antiquated event it must have been! I was too small and scared to go on most of the rides, but loved to watch, only too aware that the next day at school we would have to paint a picture entitled "My Day at the Fair".

We would all go home with a goldfish in a plastic bag. The new pets would be our pride and joy until another distraction took their place. Inevitably they would start to look a little sick, at which point Mother would take charge. They all went the same way — flushed down the toilet!

Of course not all fairs were like that. Joyce Hopkins of Liverpool recalls the day she was the local Rose Queen as a nine-year-old in 1960:

At that time annual garden fêtes were very popular at the local churches, and each year a Rose Queen would be chosen by the Sunday school. I was picked one year and I can recall how wonderful it all was. I had a retinue of four little girls and two page boys to carry my red velvet cloak, and my best friend was maid of honour.

Many weeks were spent in preparation and on the day itself we had a procession around the parish. Lorries were decorated and the Brownies, Guides, Boys' Brigade etc. all took part. We arrived at the local park where various stalls had been set out for people to browse around and enjoy. Then, after the ceremony of crowning the Rose Queen, we settled down to watch the entertainment provided by various Church organisations. The Brownies danced around the maypole, the Boys' Brigade put on a fine display of marching and everyone had a really wonderful day.

Teenage Years

The End of Innocence

TEENAGE YEARS

THE END OF INNOCENCE

Around the time that music and fashion were dominating the teenage scene I became vaguely aware that girls weren't quite as revolting as I'd always imagined. They were a bit soppy, they didn't want to come fishing, giggled a lot, and there was something they did every month that none of us were supposed to talk about, even if any of us actually knew what it was. However, at the age of about 14 I found myself more and more drawn to their company.

My teenage years were just one long drink. The first four or five years were one long drink of quite dreadful *Espresso* coffee. The following couple of years were lost in the haze of a new thing called alcohol.

Apart from on drink, our limited funds went into the juke box. We played the Beatles for hour after hour after hour. We played all the hits: *Hard Day's Night, Please Please Me, I Wanna Hold Your Hand,* and we played all those B sides like *Please Don't Wear Red Tonight* and *This Boy.* We knew all the words and we sang every single one over and over and over again. We shook our Beatle mops, and went, 'And you know you should be glad, ooooohhhhhh!' in all the right places. We knew every track of every album. I did an appearance at a disco at the end of 1989 and although the average age in that West London club was under 25, the kids still knew all the lyrics to the old Beatles albums that the DJ in the club was playing: *I'm a Loser, No Reply, Eight Days a Week* – they knew the lot.

I remember seeing them on 'Juke Box Jury' one Saturday night with the trendy young David Jacobs as the show's host, and although I was a total Beatle fanatic I have to say that they were embarrassingly unfunny. Only John (my hero) emerged with any credit. He was the only one who said anything remotely entertaining, the rest of them mumbled a lot. Somebody, presumably Brian Epstein, must have had a good 'go' at them because the next time I saw them they were on a show in America and they were absolutely brilliant. Sharp, self-mocking and witty, and the whole world loved them.

Because I was away at boarding school from the age of 13, my teenage years were a bit restricted. They were split into what I could do in the holidays and what I could get away with in term time. We used to wear our sixties clothes underneath our school uniforms whenever we went out into town. We used to hate girls seeing us in our school gear on a Monday when they'd seen us dolled up on Saturday night. We used to have to meet in the darkest of coffee bars, and later in the dirtiest of back-street pubs, to be sure that none of the masters would pop in for a pint. Mostly they were cider pubs, where we used to get completely legless on real bad old *Scrumpy* for ten old pence a pint (that's about five new pence). My girlfriend and I would have a really good night's drinking and somehow weave our way onto the bus home and pay our fares, all for less than five shillings.

We had the most elaborate systems for getting out of school after dark, even to the extreme of leaving silhouette dummies in our upstairs window to look as if we were sitting studying. We had coats with hoods, coats with high collars, woolly hats, balaclavas. A mate of mine in the sixth form was caught in town wearing a wig and a false beard. The master who reported him spotted it was him straight away because the incredibly dumb boy had his jumper on inside out with his name tag showing. He was taken back to school and given six of the Headmaster's very crisp thwacks on the botty and has presumably gone on to become a top estate agent.

In the holidays we lived life to the full. We got all the gear on to go and pose at the 'in' places in town till they closed. We were Beatles fans, we were Stones fans, we were Who fans, and I was briefly a Kink. We could go out in our wide flares and tank tops confident that we looked fabulous.

I remember thinking what a very hot and uncomfy garment the kaftan was. Boy was I glad when flower power was over, especially as kaftan wearing coincided with a couple of really hot summers.

Girls were plentiful, but they weren't quite as liberal as the sixties hype says they were supposed to be. For my mates and I the sixties were mainly a series of fumbled nights of heavy petting followed by a sudden sitting bolt upright by the girl in question and a desperate putting back on of whatever we'd managed to take off, which was usually not a lot. I spent most of the sixties getting my face slapped.

Then, if it was still open, it was back to the pub, pretending to each other that our sex lives were much more successful and varied than they really were. In the haze of drink at closing time each night we probably all believed our own brave tales as well.

Anyone who says he remembers the sixties can't have been there . . .

PARTY TIME!

What I got most was drunk. This could have been one of the main reasons for my constant rejection by young sixties' dolly birds. That and my hideously spotty face. But I have a feeling that my perpetually anti-social inebriation, causing me to fall over a lot and be sick a lot, was one of the main reasons why I didn't spend the whole of the sixties in bed with Julie Christie and Jean Shrimpton. Excessive drinking wasn't a great puller, I discovered, but, as I finally broke free of the restrictions of boarding school, it became a major part of my life. At the age of 18, most nights were spent having a few early ones in the university bar and then weaving around Birmingham drinking pint after pint in any pub silly enough to still serve us.

We were always looking for parties and amazingly there always seemed to be one. Addresses were furtively handed across on crumpled bits of paper and off we'd all go to try and gatecrash, clutching one bottle of Ansells' brown ale each. Frequently, because we never took girls with us, we weren't welcome.

EXPRESS YOURSELF

'Teenagers' were invented in the fifties. Before then they had been regarded as spotty oiks, stranded somewhere between childhood and being grown up. In the United States people realised here was a whole new kind of person, who wanted clothes, records, make-up, concert tickets, jeans, *Coca Cola*, hamburgers, you name it, and who didn't need to spend their money on anything other than having a good time.

In Britain the first of these fashion-conscious individuals gathered in tribes — Teddy Boys, Beatniks, Mods, Rockers and various sub-species of girls as well as boys — who dressed alike, ran in packs and fought their rivals in famous Bank Holiday punch-ups.

And with the ending of National Service in Britain, the last batch of 18-year-olds were called up in November 1960, which meant that there were a lot more young men around to don a different kind of uniform — depending on which youth tribe they aspired to . . .

To Peter Alvey of Nottinghamshire, doing National Service was like attending the University of Life:

My papers arrived as a cunningly worded invitation to a get-together the War Office was having at Catterick.

There we were taught to swear like well troopers and drink until we were unwell troopers, before finally passing out as masters of the technique of charming the knickers off a nun.

By the mid fifties the establishment had lost a lot of its credibility. Firstly over the Burgess, Maclean and Philby spy incidents, and then over the Suez crisis. From it grew the age of the Angry Young Man, and a crop of writers under the age of 30 emerged who stuck two fingers up at the establishment and showed their dissent. Influential books and plays from this period include: *Lucky Jim* by Kingsley Amis; John Osborne's *Look Back in Anger*; *Room at the Top* by John Braine; and then there was Alan Sillitoe's *Saturday Night and Sunday Morning*. — The film version had the audacity to use the word 'arse' on the silver screen. It was a major censorship breakthrough and the character Arthur Seaton was one of the new self-styled local scoundrel heroes that many teenagers modelled themselves on.

Estelle P Farrell of Liverpool (fifties) remembers:

I was by now a Teddy Girl with blonde hair and a DA haircut. I was great at the "bop" — a kind of dance. Another dance was the "creep", a slowie. Clothes-wise, we didn't have a lot: long, straight skirts with slits either side or down the front, thin polo neck sweaters with chiffon straps, three-quarter length jackets (swing backs). I had a red gaberdine zoot suit which I made for my sister's wedding at a cost of £6. I wore stockings with butterflies or roses up the sides and waspie belts.

In the fifties the angry young men became Teddy Boys, those guys who sought gang warfare (forerunners of the modern-day lager lout). They were easily recognisable in their draped jackets, with velvet collar, shoelace ties, drainpipe trousers, luminous socks, and crêpe soled shoes. Invariably they each had a Teddy Girl complete with the statutory 12-in bouffon hairstyle, wide-hemmed dress and four-in stiletto shoes.

The aggressive image of Teddy Boys resulted in an increase in crime, and offences by persons under the age of 21 doubled in the latter half of the fifties.

Even a respectable suited chap wanted to be a working class hero — you know, swear a bit and kick up a fuss about the establishment. Only thing was, on telly the hero managed to crack the system — we just got arrested.

Yeah, well, you had to keep the Mods in line, didn't you? We didn't take no aggro from smoothies in two-tone suits. Call them Vespas motorbikes? Mind you, you had to keep a look-out for the police — they were on to who dunnit pretty fast.

Teddy Boys were replaced by Rockers in the sixties. These were the guys who used to terrorise local communities by roaring through towns and villages on their 500 Nortons creating as much noise as they could on the way. But with the fashion boom there arrived the polo neck sweater and kaftan coat brigade, the Mods, who were not to be outdone by the Rockers although somehow they didn't quite have the same impact on their Vespas and Lambrettas. But when the two sets of rivals met, like that day at Margate on 18th May 1964, it was warfare.

Tricia Reed lived in Dartford, Kent, in 1964 and remembers vividly that day of shame at Margate:

In the mid sixties I became a Mod. I dressed in Hush Puppy shoes with lace-ups, a three-quarter length suede coat, wore my hair very short indeed and used pale, ghost-like, lipstick.

On May 18th 1964, my boyfriend and I, dressed in our Mod gear, visited the seaside at Margate. It was a Bank Holiday Monday and we had to go there by train as his Lambretta scooter was being repaired. We wandered around the town for a while and then decided to head for the beach. By this time the number of Mods and Rockers on the beach had out-numbered the general public who had come for a bit of peace and quiet. Before we knew what was happening a fight had broken out with deck chairs and bottles being thrown around. Suddenly the police appeared and tried to quell the situation, which only aggravated us even more. A lot of people got hurt in the ensuing riot. By this time I was really frightened and wanted to go home.

There wasn't the same emphasis on clothes in the early fifties as there was in the latter part of the decade or in the sixties. ICI made a major breakthrough in clothing manufacture in 1950 when it announced that its new factory at Redcar would be manufacturing a new fabric called *Terylene*. A full-skirted frock in tweed-like jersey with a dog's-tooth check cost more than the norm in 1950 at £5 6s (£5.30). 20 years later, with such a boom in clothing and fashion, girls were paying only £3 for mass-produced lines like C&A teenage 'A' line dresses.

Margaret Woodhouse of Nottinghamshire:

We used to soak our underskirts in a mixture of sugar and water to make them really stand out under our full skirts.

. . . and for some people those never-to-be-forgotten days couldn't come quickly enough, as Tricia Reed remembers:

At the age of ten, in about 1957, all of us girls started to measure our chests to see if we needed a bra. At last, 18 months later, I attained the magic 28 in bust and bought my first bra in Woolworths for the sum of 1s 9d (8p). I rushed home to put it on — what a disappointment. It was so uncomfortable and didn't fit at all well. The worst problem was having to tell Mum as she had to wash it for me, and it shrunk in the wash. But it was worth it I felt so grown up.

Waiting to catch a glimpse of her hero a girl never knew when she might need a little extra support — and if it wasn't found in the arms of a policeman then America's fashion favourite bra would do the trick — with or without floating action . . .

But as the fifties progressed, teenagers became more rebellious. They didn't want to be like their parents. They wanted their own identity and one person who went a long way towards giving them that was Mary Quant. She knew girls no longer wanted to dress like their mothers, and so with a variety of bright colours and new materials she produced contemporary styles which rocked Britain.

Mrs J Davey of Bristol did her growing up between 1953 and 1963 and remembers how important it was to wear fashionable clothing:

It was difficult with no money of your own to persuade your mother how important it was to be fashionably dressed. I was allowed to wear stockings for "best" — how I hated the feel of them and those awful suspenders, but I put up with the suffering as it was "grown up". I wasn't allowed make-up so the bright red Woolworths lipstick was applied in the phone box and removed before I went home. Skirts had by now become very full, with layers of petticoats and nipped-in waists. I was really too plump to do this particular fashion justice but would never have admitted it at the time! I remember short white gloves and my first pair of high heels, or rather very little Louis heels, but at least they made the right noise when you walked, which was the important thing!

I can't remember women wearing trousers although I believe I did have some revolting plaid "trews" for casual wear. On holiday "short shorts" were all the rage.

Heels on shoes eventually got higher and thinner and the stiletto was the curse of your mother's linoleum and the local dance hall floor. Hemlines were slowly creeping up and up. Soon the mini emerged with long white PVC boots, and stockings were replaced by pantie hose.

As skirts went up, tights went down a treat — all in the best possible taste. And true Beatles fans weren't afraid to wear their hearts on their sleeves — or dresses, for that matter.

127

NICE LEGS

Along with future husband Alexander Plunket-Greene and Archie McNair, Mary Quant opened their first Bazaar boutique in London's King's Road in 1955, and a second in Knightsbridge in 1961.

New fabrics like *Crimplene* made the mass production of these new clothes that much easier and teenage girls used the fashion boom as a means of spending their spare cash and also creating their own identity. Of course, the mini skirt replaced the long flowing skirts of the fifties and projected the new promiscuous image of the decade. The feminine look of the fifties was gone, and the sensual look of the sixties had arrived with models like Twiggy and Jean Shrimpton flaunting the new image.

The mini was eventually followed by the midi and then maxi skirt at the end of the decade and trouser suits became popular with girls.

Today's teenagers tend to think they invented denim jeans but they may be surprised to learn that in 1955 jeans had already become the number one selling style for women.

Possibly the only time in history when less might cost you more . . . Skirts shortened and legs went on show — but you did have to keep your legs awfully close together. We had lots of interesting discussions about the Stones' latest album, latest single, latest concert . . . Funny, the blokes never seemed to feel over dressed.

After Mary Quant's Bazaar came Biba boutiques. If you looked like Barbara Hulanicki then Biba could supply your entire wardrobe – though a few hat tricks never went amiss.

Diana Davis of Bristol confirms the popularity of jeans in the fifties:

It is funny to recall that denim trousers have long been part of our culture. I can remember wearing a pair over 40 years ago, but in those days we called them "pedal-pushers" and one of the neighbours commented that it was quite shameful to see young girls dressed in this fashion!

But it was not only the girls who became fashion conscious; the boys also wanted to make sure they wore the latest clothes: cuban heeled boots, polo neck sweaters and ice blue jeans. And it was thanks to Glaswegian John Stephen that Carnaby Street was born and London became the fashion centre of the world in the sixties.

There was a considerable Italian influence on clothing in Britain, particularly on hair styles, shoes and suits. There were 15,000 Italian immigrations to Britain between the end of the war and 1951, and the immigrants brought their clothing styles with them. Many of them got work in catering establishments and consequently their influence spread. Many of the coffee bars became great meeting places for kids in the fifties and sixties as they would sit over one cup of *Espresso* coffee or a bottle of *Coke* for hours listening to the latest sounds from the pop charts blaring out from the juke box in the corner.

How Chris Marsh of Newport longed for the day when he could eventually go to his local Italian café in the early sixties:

The small Italian café in the centre of my home town of Blaenavon was, for a small boy of five in the early sixties, a palace of delights, with vast rows of jars of sweets, the most delicious home-made ice-cream, and the mysterious sound of the Espresso coffee machine. But above all, I remember the growing aware-ness that it was, after the five o'clock curfew imposed by my parents, the focal point for those nasty boys who wore leather jackets and rode motor bikes.

It was some years before I plucked up the courage to enter that post-five o'clock den of iniquity. I marched boldly past the sweet counter and the tables full of glaring, long-haired youths and, with pounding heart and a sweating hand clutching at some small change (which was very big change to me in those days), I made straight for the juke box.

I remember the names of those magic artists with great nostalgia: Jethro Tull, John Mayall, Fleetwood Mac . . . I fed the machine my shilling piece for which I was entitled to make five selections. I pressed A4 to hear The Driving Song *which was the 'B' side of Jethro Tull's* Living in the Past *and I remember realising that this was heaven. And my choice of music seemed to gain me a small degree of acceptance amongst these older children whom I saw as men.*

Leisure time wasn't sports filled as it is now. We girls would meet at home and sit for hours in the bedroom, the walls covered with posters of pop stars, talking endlessly — about clothes, boys, bands . . .

A great deal of attention was placed on hair styles by both boys and girls. If a boy didn't have a good old-fashioned short back and sides, it is a good bet he had either *Brylcreem*ed-back hair with a DA (the sides were brushed back to meet down the middle to create the DA, or duck's arse), a Tony Curtis quiff, or a crew cut, thus confirming the American influence this side of the Atlantic.

Women opted for the beehive which was often forced to stay in place with a mixture of sugar and water by those who couldn't afford the ozone-layer-shattering aerosols (not that we'd heard of the ozone layer in the sixties).

Mrs J Davey of Bristol (early sixties):

Every night I slept in rollers; next morning lengthy back-combing was necessary to turn the eventual sculptured look into a "beehive", "cottage loaf" or "French pleat". The whole lot was finished off with a heavy spray of lacquer which took the polish off your dressing table and ruined the bathroom mirror.

But with the dawning of the sixties there came short hair for the girls and long hair for the boys as the Beatles and other pop groups became trendsetters. The Beatles in particular brought with them their distinctive haircuts and innovative lapel-less jackets with round necks.

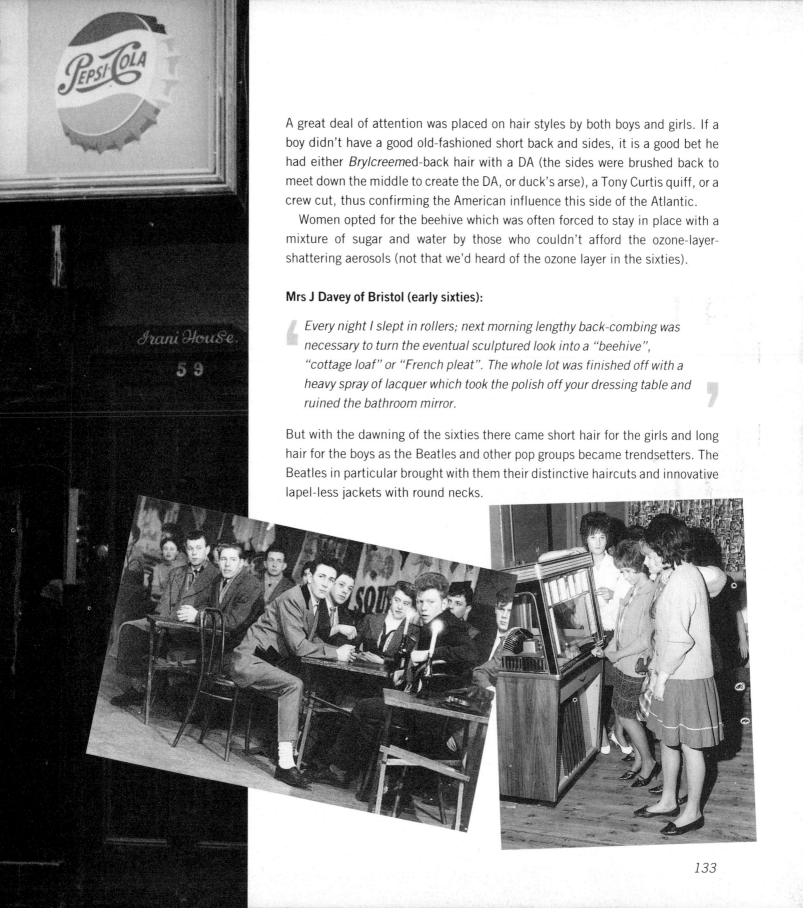

Estelle Farrell lived in Liverpool at the time of the pop boom of the early sixties but she was otherwise occupied:

I left school at the age of 15 and worked in a button factory, which I hated, for £1 5s (£1.25) a week. There were plenty of jobs after that one but for low money. I then went to work in a teashop baking bread, cakes and pies. In the afternoon I'd push the owner's baby around Prince's Park in her pram. I used to deposit the week's takings (amounting to £40) at the bank (I now earned £1 10s (£1.50) a week). I left there to work at a big bakers in town for 5s (25p) more. I used to go to work on my bike in pedal pushers, calf-length pants like a matador's with buttons on the sides of the calves. Then I got married at 17 and was having babies until 1965, so although I would have loved being a flower child in the sixties I couldn't very well, what with five children to drag around.

By the end of the fifties the youths were affluent. They had full-time employment and plenty of money to spend. A report published in August 1959 reckoned the average working male youth earned £8 per week and had £5 per week to spend on clothes, cigarettes and records. In addition, girls spent a lot of their spare cash on cosmetics which helped to take the British teenager's spending over £800 million per annum. For the first time the marketing men had a mass target area and so they concentrated on the teenager.

Helen Severn of Nottinghamshire didn't have a great deal left out of her first week's wages:

At the end of the fifties I left school to start work in an office and earned £2 5s 3d (£2.26) per week. I had rather unattractive white sock marks on my legs for some time because we hadn't been allowed to wear stockings to school.

Teenagers in the fifties were nowhere near as permissive as their counterparts of a decade later. Sex was not taught in schools and sex before marriage was very unusual. As a consequence, people were marrying younger!

Estelle Farrell remembers her Liverpool days in the fifties:

We didn't drink and taking drugs was unheard of. We did see a lot of fights though, with bottles, razors and bike chains. We used to get what was called a "tail home": The lads would all stand in a group and eye the girls and at the last dance they would ask for a dance and then offer to take you home. We must have been mad, but there wasn't any sex like now.

Well, maybe some were a bit promiscuous in the fifties; Peter Alvey of Nottinghamshire, for example, recalls moments from the summer of 1959:

A memorable week in Yarmouth, the Queen of towns on the Norfolk coast, where each sun-scorched day started on a low with a shocking hangover and achieved a nightly high around the stocking tops. Conquests were only marred by the fear of the faulty one in ten condom.

Oh where are you now, you femmes fatales, Daphne, Jill, Pauline and Sylvia? Somewhere in your unfamished fat fifties I guess.

The sixties era was totally different, it became the age of promiscuity. The youth of the day had seen and heard about the war years and decided they would rather 'Make Love, Not War'. In January 1961 the birth control pill went on sale in the United Kingdom and was available on prescription from 1963. The Pill caused a great deal of controversy in the Vatican and Pope Paul VI condemned it as 'an act against the will of God'. By 1966 illegitimate births had nearly doubled over the last ten years. Perhaps the Pill came too late? Thanks to the efforts of David Steel, the Abortion Bill was passed by Parliament in 1967 and from 27th April 1963 legalised abortions were permitted in the United Kingdom. In December 1969 the Family Planning Association opened its second vasectomy clinic in Birmingham (the first was opened in Cardiff some time earlier). It was a snip at £16 a go!

Some lay the blame for the promiscuity of the era on Dr Spock's *The Common Sense Book of Baby and Child Care* because it encouraged parents of the fifties to relax traditional controls and let children have their own way.

The Liverpool experience is further recalled by Pauline Hartley who remembers those early sixties days:

We used to wear full swing skirts and tops with Cliff Richard embroidered lovingly across them, pale frosted lipstick and pointed flatties or Louis heeled shoes. We didn't have much money, but had enough to buy a bottle of pop and go on the Waltzers at New Brighton Fair. We were perfectly happy. We would walk along the promenade from Seacombe ferry and if any boys tried to talk to us we would laugh girlishly.

In the early sixties I went to the Tower Ballroom at New Brighton to see the Beatles. I actually sat on the edge of the stage at John Lennon's feet! Many stars used to perform there and we'd totter in with our high heels and big handbags. The world was full of magic and romance, or so we thought.

The sixties was undoubtedly the greatest era for pop music in Britain. But it was only thanks to the likes of Elvis Presley and Bill Haley, exponents of rock and roll, that Tommy Steele, Cliff Richard and Adam Faith were spawned. Britain went crazy and the sounds of *Poor Me*, *Fall in Love with You* and *A White Sports Coat* were heard coming out of every juke box in every coffee bar, the new social centre of the universe.

And one such coffee bar user was Mrs J Davey of Bristol:

The pop scene was in full bloom and as I entered my teens I rapidly got caught up in it. I had left friends in the village behind now and often spent the weekend with friends in town or bribed my father to come and pick me up. I spent hours mooning around stage doors, autograph hunting and writing "I love Tommy [Steele]" all over my school books. As I got older we used to go to coffee bars and hang around the juke box or sit in rows hand jiving.

Jim Finn, Liverpool (mid fifties):

In the mid fifties Bill Haley and Elvis Presley caused a revolution in music and clothes for teenagers who began to thumb their noses at grown-up, fuddy-duddy customs and traditions. When Lonnie Donegan invented skiffle, hundreds of musical DIY-ers bought or borrowed a guitar, which sowed the seeds of the later Mersey beat era.

C A Garrett of Bristol recalls that the youth culture of the fifties revolved round music:

It was the mid fifties and we 15-year-olds were leaving school and entering into a very sober Britain. Our social lives consisted of visits to the cinema, the youth club above the Co-op or the showground. The showground was our favourite with its flashing lights and music belting out loudly.

We were young and bursting with excitement, looking for music we could whirl and twirl to. Sure enough it was on its way. With the arrival of Bill Haley and the Comets the youth of Britain erupted into the age of Rock and Roll and life was never the same again. Next came the one we had all been waiting for: Elvis, of course. We screamed, we rocked, and when his first film came to Bristol it was as if every teenager in town had descended on the cinema. The queues stretched for miles. As soon as he appeared on the screen everyone left their seats and screamed so loudly not a word he said could be heard. The manager tried to restore order but it was impossible. We listened to Jerry Lee Lewis, Fats Domino, Little Richard and countless others twanging their guitars.

Britain answered with some great music, the best being Cliff Richard. The fifties had set a precedent and music continued to be a very large part of teenage cult life.

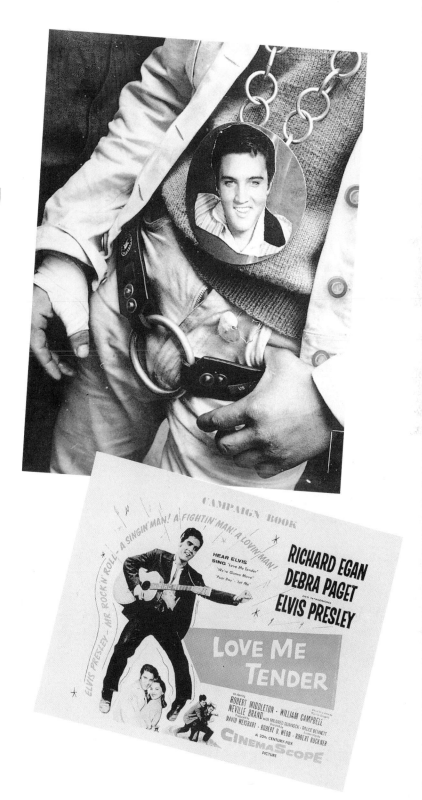

All day we'd swap news and views on our favourite bands, living and breathing through our idols, imitating their clothes and hair styles and dreaming of a similar life style.

MUSIC MANIA

To cater for the teenage and pop boom, television provided pop programmes like 'Oh Boy', 'Six, Five Special', 'Thank Your Lucky Stars' and 'Juke Box Jury' — all compulsive viewing for the teenager of the day. And of course there was still the radio, which by now was no longer called a wireless. It had a new name, transistor, or tranny for short. And from these new pocket-sized electronic wonders came the sounds of the sixties from Radio Luxembourg, while Tony Blackburn and Simon Dee broadcast from their pirate radio station, Radio Caroline, moored off the coast near Harwich. Radio and television coverage of the pop scene was complemented by the constant playing of 45s on the record player, normally a Dansette, Murphy or Bush.

Of course parents were up in arms. They thought their children were wasting their time, and indeed money, on records. And how they abhorred the likes of Mick Jagger. 'Disgusting!' they cried. But, in reality, the success of the pop boom of the early sixties stemmed from the fact that many parents actually liked the music that the Beatles and the likes produced.

As the early sixties arrived, the pop music scene was starting to become stale. On 3rd February 1959 Buddy Holly had been killed in a plane crash, and many referred to the date as 'the day the music died'. That is until the arrival of the Beatles, who shot up the charts with *Please Please Me* in 1963. Like Elvis Presley in the States, they brought a new sound and dimension to the pop world. Others emulated them with great success: the Dave Clark Five, Gerry and the Pacemakers and the Rolling Stones, to mention just three notable groups of those early pioneering days of the pop boom.

Brian Birchall was another of those teenagers lucky enough to be living in Liverpool in the early sixties:

Being a teenager in Liverpool in the sixties must have been one of the most happy times, if not the happiest, of my life. The city was alive with music and fashion. When I was 15 and working in the city centre I would go down to the Cavern with my mates for a lunchtime session (admission 2s 6d – 12p), stay for a couple of hours and end up losing my job when I returned late for work. Little did I know that the groups we saw then would become musical giants: the Beatles, Gerry and the Pacemakers, Searchers, Swinging Blue Jeans, etc. The other main club in the city, the Iron Door in Temple Street, was another venue where the atmosphere was incredible. Even when we went to the Cavern for an all-nighter (24 hour dance) it wasn't possible to buy an alcoholic drink – only soft drinks. We were 18 then but nobody minded because people were more interested in what was happening around them. The Mods with their Parka coats complete with The Who motifs on the backs, and Vespa scooters, would congregate at the Pier Head. The girls all had Mary Quant hair styles, pan stick make-up and eyes like Dusty Springfield, thick with black mascara.

Anything to do with music had to be a success in the sixties. They were all-singing, all-dancing times, when we lived for the next gig and just twisted the nights away.

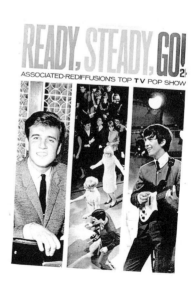

DANCIN' THE NIGHT AWAY

The large dance halls of the fifties were turned into pop music emporiums where thousands of screaming fans could drool over their idols of the day. But the Locarnos of this world still really belonged to the parents. Consequently, new-found places of entertainment had to be found. Clubs like the Cavern in Liverpool and London's Marquee Club became new havens for music fans who were entertained for hours by live groups, all of whom were hopeful of becoming the next chart-toppers. Clubs like the Cavern were dark, dingy, sweaty and loud. But what wonderful places they were.

Liverpool was unquestionably the place to be in the early sixties as Alice O'Hagan recalls:

I was 13 years old in 1962 and had two older sisters. We were allowed to go to the local dance hall, the Locarno Ballroom, but Jean and I had to be home early. Monday night was record night and as I was not allowed to wear make-up I had to wait until I arrived at the "Loc" before applying my mask. I would make a frantic dash to the Ladies' boudoir, terrified in case any of the local lads saw me without my "eyes" on.

All the girls' make-up bags would be opened simultaneously. Out would come the Miners blue eyeshadow, the Rimmel liquid eyeliner, the Max Factor black mascara . . . Then it was straight to the dance floor with the revolving crystal ball overhead. We had just learnt to do the Shadow walk so Jean and I wanted to show off.

The memory of Jean and I running like the clappers all the way home, whilst trying to erase the make-up, never fails to bring a smile to my face. If my father had ever discovered any left-over traces of make-up, we would have been confined to barracks for a week.

Elaine Peggs from London recalls the days of early fifties dance halls before trendy fashions and 'pop' music:

In 1952 nearly everyone went dancing on a Saturday night. Saturday afternoons would find me with a face pack on, soaking in the bath. Then there was the ritual of painting my nails before dressing "coolly" in my gaberdine dress. Hundreds of other girls were doing the same. Meanwhile, the boys were donning their finger-tip drape suits, crêpe-soled shoes (beetle crushers), smart shirts and narrow ties.

Each October the major swimming pool at East Ham Town Hall was drained and covered with a sprung dance floor for the next six months. It was the most exciting place you could imagine. Now when we go to the Over 50s club I have only to step through the doors and sniff the air and I'm transported back in time.

143

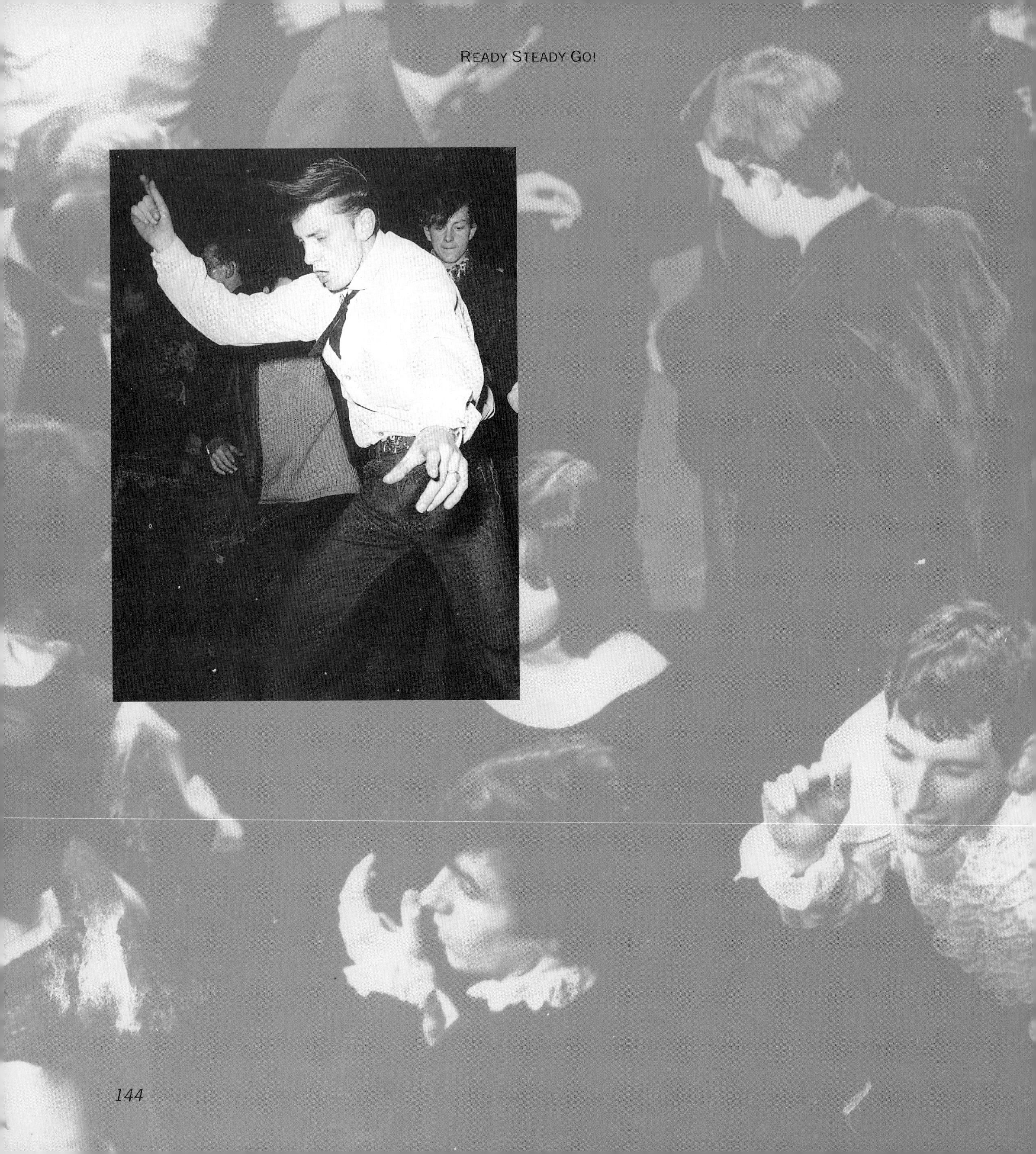

From the days of Bill Haley's Rock Around the Clock, *on 78 of course, dancing became less of a contact pastime and by the sixties couples gyrated on the dance floor 'doing their own thing' and contact was very rare.*

FLOWER POWER

By 1967 Flower Power and its 'lovely people' dominated the teenage scene and clothes changed to suit the mood of the era. It was the day of the Hippie with 'anything goes' clothing, and drugs and sex were prevalent as the motto of 'Make Love, Not War' had a stronger feeling than at the start of the decade. On the music scene that year the Beatles' revolutionary LP *Sergeant Pepper's Lonely Hearts Club Band* made more than a fleeting reference to drugs.

But, as a 20-year-old, Bob Reed of Dartford wanted to find out about Flower Power first-hand in the United States:

The early sixties' TV shows from America, particularly "Route 66" and "77 Sunset Strip", left a deep impression on my mind. I had a passion to see the places for myself, so I went to San Francisco and Los Angeles that summer. The whole country seemed to be on the verge of a youth rebellion. I wrote excited letters back home to my girlfriend full of expressions like "far out", "freaky", "turned on", "drop out" and so on. I thought this was only happening in America but on returning home to England the same atmosphere existed. It was as if the whole world was possessed by Flower Power. It seemed a magical time that would never end.

After all the energy we put into the early part of the decade, in the late sixties it was cool to be laid back. We hung around doing and wearing what we felt like, feelin' groovy and letting it all hang loose somewhere far out on cloud nine.

During a decade when the youngster took very little seriously and wanted to express individualism, the atmosphere of the day spread throughout all cultural forms. The art world was not exempt from the changing face of Britain in the sixties. And so was born Pop Art which gave us pictures of Heinz beans tins or *Brillo* pads courtesy of Messrs Warhol and Hockney, and it was Warhol who gave us those wonderful life-size pictures of Marilyn Monroe which still adorn bedroom and living room walls up and down the country. Freedom of expression and the use of colour gave Hockney and Warhol the chance to escape from reality, which was something all teenagers sought, and still do.

Paul Laver of Bristol sums up being a sixties' teenager:

A feeling in the air, unseen, intangible . . . perhaps the wind of change blowing. The year was 1963 and I was 14 years old, sheltered and a dreamer. The following seven years were tailor-made for a dreamer.

The awakening came for me when a schoolfriend suggested we go along to see a group from London. At the concert I went to the toilet. As I was combing my hair in the mirror, two men walked in. At first I thought they were girls. They wore high-necked paisley shirts buttoned down at the collar, checked jackets with long vents and black flared trousers with very high Cuban heels. They reminded me of 18th century dandies. I was knocked out by the look. The two men in the toilet were Ray and Dave Davies of the Kinks. The music they played was raw and so different to anything I had heard before. I was hooked.

I was terribly shy, but in a short space of time I became a rebel dressed in a guard's jacket with gold epaulettes, silver crushed velvet trousers, white plimsolls and fur gloves. I also found a girlfriend. I had arrived.

WORLD AROUND US

FROM RATIONING TO THE MOON

WORLD AROUND US

FROM RATIONING TO THE MOON

" *For most of us as we grew up, the great enemy became Russia. There had been the great purge of communists in America and the airlift to Berlin, but although our comics — like the* Hotspur *and the* Eagle *— still carried wartime strips in which we fought the Germans (and of course always won), Russia was emerging as the country we were most likely to have to fight in the next war. I suppose we expected war really. It had been 10 or 15 years and I think most of us thought something would flare up soon.* "

I think I was just about five years old, so details are vague, but I remember the Headmaster came in halfway through the first lesson after lunch and whispered something in our form mistress's car. The next thing I was home with my Mummy in time for a second lunch. Apparently the King had died, and the pretty Princess Elizabeth was now the Queen of England. Someone called Hillary, a funny name I thought for a man, climbed up the biggest mountain in the world a few days before the Queen's Coronation.

As I grew up in the fifties the world was still pretty much unchanged since the end of the war. Ten years after the signing of the peace treaty with Germany there were still mementoes of the war everywhere. Dad regularly went to meetings of ex-soldiers. They were called MOTHs (the Memorable Order of Tin Hats), and the get-togethers were mainly an excuse for celebrating the fact that they were still alive after all, and getting absolutely legless. Most houses had war memorabilia on the mantelpiece. There'd be photos of the man or men of the house in full uniform, with messages like, 'I'll be home soon, my darling' written at the bottom of the frame. Of course in many cases they did not come home soon, and ten years later the man of the house was someone completely different. I remember this puzzling me a lot when I was young. I couldn't work out why Uncle Jack looked so very different during the war. In later life it turned out that Uncle Jack was still Uncle

Jack but the man in the old photograph had been Uncle David, who was killed at Arnhem.

I also discovered quite young that the men who talked most about the war had never been anywhere near it. Most of my Dad's close friends had fought right through from Dunkirk to D-Day and his brother had been out in the jungle fighting the Japanese. They all went off and got steaming drunk together at MOTHs, but they didn't talk about the war at all, never mentioned it. The ones who came round to our house and kept on and on about it had usually been nowhere more dangerous than Eastbourne.

There was also a lot of German memorabilia in peoples' houses. We had a huge German shell which for many years served as an umbrella stand, a German medal, the Iron Cross, and a Swastika flag. For many years I was a bit worried about which side Dad had actually fought on.

The war gradually seemed to fade from most memories, at least on the surface. I just about remember the last of the ration books and people moaning about how little their war bonds were worth when they cashed them in. There were furniture dockets, and men who sold clothes at your door getting you deeply into long term debt, called Tallymen. Soldiers were still a familiar sight, and National Service was a normal part of every family's life. The sons disappeared for two years at a time, coming back every few months looking muscular and shaven headed, and always wore their uniforms when they went to dances. There was a series of emergencies which mums with National Service soldiers in their families prayed their sons wouldn't be sent to. There was something in Borneo and Cyprus and Aden and Suez and Korea. The woman in the next street had a son killed by the Mau Mau in Kenya.

There are so many odd scattered images that crowd my mind about that frenetic 20 years. I remember our school being taken to visit a little camp of escapees from the Hungarian uprising in 1956. They were wrapped in blankets and had dead eyes which stared in front of them without registering the arrival of us children at all, as if they had seen things too awful to ever tell. Then there was the bitter cold winter of 1963 and the huge slide we built in our park that led to at least five children breaking their arms in a single day. The Thames was so solid with ice that the local paper carried a picture of a double-decker bus driving across the river to an island in the middle.

SHOCKS AND SURPRISES

There was Christopher Craig's picture in the paper when he became the last man to be hanged in this country. The Great Train Robbery! . . . The Krays and when they came to Birmingham to try and take over the nightclub scene in the Midlands.

There was the shock as details emerged of the Moors Murders. I remember John McVicar, and Charles Manson and his disciples horrifically murdering Sharon Tate.

Or what about the excitement when the M1 opened, and how a newsreel that night showed one lonely Ford Consul using the middle lane? The Minister asked us to make more use of it. Sitting in yet another solid ten mile traffic jam in the nineties, I wished he'd never asked.

I remember a free submarine that you got inside cereal packets that only worked if you filled it with baking powder.

I remember us winning the World Cup and thinking Martin Peters was the most talented man in the world.

I remember the night Cassius Clay beat Sonny Liston, and I remember him being stripped of his title because he wouldn't fight in Vietnam.

I remember Pete Murray and Cathy McGowan and David Jacobs and 'Juke Box Jury', 'Ready, Steady, Go!' and 'Six Five Special' and Wally Whyton and Ollie Beak.

I remember the Ted Taylor Trio and Don Lang and his Frantic Five. I remember Mu Young and Neil Young.

And somehow in the same little space of years I remember a man landed on the moon . . .

A classic character of the fifties was the tearaway, the moody guy in the black leather jacket who would have endless rows with his parents and scrapes with the law. He was to be found in countless TV plays and films.

The equally classic excuse for such behaviour was 'Well we're all living in the shadow of the bomb – if we're all going to die, I'm going to get my kicks first.'

In a way it was a true threat. In the fifties and sixties the spectre of nuclear war dominated world affairs, and in Britain the Campaign for Nuclear Disarmament marched and demonstrated to remind everybody just how deadly the newly-developed hydrogen bomb might prove if it were ever to be used.

Easter 1958 saw 3,000 CND protesters marching from London to Aldermaston – by 1963, 70,000 protesters were making the trip.

Paula Donald of Manchester remembers getting her black and white Ban the Bomb badge:

Like many youngsters I joined local Ban the Bomb marches. Although too young to realise the full implications of such weaponry, many of us were frightened of another world war in our lifetime, knowing it would end many lives.

Meanwhile, real-life shooting wars were claiming lives from the Middle East to Biafra, while television brought terrible images of napalmed villages and starving children into everyone's homes.

Television covered the USA's involvement in Vietnam from the beginning. What they saw on their suburban TV screens alienated a generation who would rather burn their draft cards than go to fight a war they saw as pointless.

In the United States and Europe, protest against the bomb turned into outrage over Vietnam.

Television also brought the terror of President Kennedy's assassination, as it happened, into British homes. But television also recorded the triumphs of the time,

culminating on Moon Night, July 21st 1969, when the whole world wondered at how clever the human race seemed to be – and how fragile and vulnerable was that blue globe spinning through space.

The invasion of Hungary by Soviet troops in 1956 and the nationalisation of the Suez Canal the same year were two incidents which brought the world to the brink of another full-scale war. The Russian invasion of Czechoslovakia in 1968 also had world leaders sitting on the edge of their seats.

Mark Watts of Liverpool had his own reason for remembering the Suez crisis:

I was about eight then and remember the Suez crisis being on television all the time. I didn't know what it was about but remember my Mum and Dad talking about it a lot, so it must have been serious. But just how serious it really was came home to me when my Dad told me we wouldn't be able to go to Crosby anymore (every week we used to pack a picnic and get in the black sit-up-and-beg Ford Popular for a day trip to Crosby beach). But we carried on going. My grandfather, a Hackney cab driver in Liverpool, would come to our house on a Sunday morning and my Dad would syphon petrol out of the taxi and into our car. I didn't have a clue what was happening at the time, but of course it was all to do with the petrol crisis over Suez. I remember drinking petrol which my Dad left lying around in a pop bottle.

There were also some dreadful natural disasters like the flooding at Lynmouth in 1952 which claimed 36 lives; the Manchester United air crash at Munich on 6th February 1958, which wiped out the finest football team in England; the smog of 1962 which killed 62; the Aberfan disaster of 1966 which decimated a mining community; and the foot and mouth epidemic which ruined many farmers.

Sometimes we could run down to the High Street and watch the Aldermaston marchers go past. It all seemed very solemn and very sombre, which just made the threat of the horrifically fascinating H-Bomb even more sinister.

FROM FEAR TO SANITY

MAKE FRIENDS NOT ENEMIES

NO H-BOMBS FOR BRITAIN

BOMBS FOR BRITAIN U.S.A. RUSSIA

NO H-BOMBS FOR BRITAIN

NUCLEAR DISARMAMENT

NO TO NUCLEAR SUICIDE

FOR THE SAKE OF CHILDREN EVERYWHERE

> *It was really too cold to shape snowballs with icy wet gloves but we had to so we could put them down the boys' backs. When we got to school my hands were too numb to join together for prayers, my feet tingled like they were going to fall off, there was a smell of iciness as snow fell off balaclavas and a trail of wetness in the classrooms from wellies. It was like we lived in the North Pole and had always lived there. We got totally used to waking up to frozen milk on the doorstep and going to bed with coats on top of blankets.*

Happily it was not all gloom and disaster in the fifties and sixties: the Coronation was a joyous occasion for the British people as thousands filled the streets of London on 2nd June 1953 to celebrate the crowning of the new Queen. Those lucky few with television sets had a houseful of friends and relatives to watch the great occasion.

Margaret Stafford of Gateshead didn't have a television, but she remembers the occasion as if it was yesterday:

> *Some of the neighbours organised weekly raffles to collect money for our street party. Our street had only recently been electrified and my parents were among the first to own a refrigerator, so we became the custodians of boiled ham stored in readiness.*
>
> *The whole family, including Dad, listened to the Coronation on the wireless, remarking that poor Richard Dimbleby was drying up describing the Abbey scene before the Queen arrived. We had to wait to see the newsreel footage at the cinema, as no one we knew had a television set.*
>
> *Because of the rain, three streets combined to have their party in Beech Street mission hall. We ate our cakes and sandwiches at long tables and then the older folks danced to records.*

And then there were atrocious man-made disasters like the Sharpeville Massacre of 1960 which saw 56 blacks murdered; the Charles Manson killings of 1969 and the horrendous Moors Murders of the early sixties.

Susan Nichol of Wigan recalls Aberfan:

> *We went to a little school in a mining area near Wigan and I remember coming home to see the dreadful scenes of the Aberfan disaster on television. I didn't usually watch much serious stuff but I remember thinking to myself that it could have been me or Jane, my best friend, in that accident. It left a lasting impression on me.*

There was also that dreadful winter of 1962-63 which caused the loss of much livestock, did millions of pounds worth of damage to roads and property, made the unemployment figures rise and played absolute havoc with sporting fixtures.

. . . and Mrs Jennifer Farquhar (then Jennifer Jane Thomson) of the Wirral will never forget the Coronation Coat of Arms:

> *Queen Elizabeth's Coronation in 1953 is a dim memory, but I was given a mug and remember that red, white and blue were the "in" colours for dresses, socks and hair ribbons. One of the magazines must have issued a transfer to commemorate the occasion because I still have the picture of the Coat of Arms embroidered by my Mum. It was really a sampler and at the bottom were the words, "I made this in 1953 to commemorate the Coronation of our dear Queen Elizabeth II for Jennifer Jane Thomson."*

Ann Harwood of Somerset also has dim memories of the Coronation, but the mug was not forgotten:

> *My memories of the Queen's Coronation are quite vague as I was only four years old, but I remember we had red, white and blue flowers all around the border of the garden. I was also jealous of my brother who was at school and getting a Coronation mug, so Mum had to go to the Co-op and buy one for me. She also made a cardigan for my doll in red, white and blue stripes.*

The winter of 1963 was a real cracker. While all the grown-ups fumed about the problems of getting to work or a few hours' honest toil with a broom, a shovel and a trip to the coal-bunker allowed us to build the best snowmen ever.

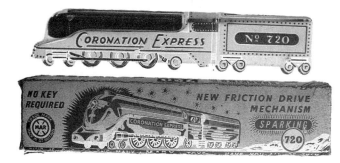

We danced in the streets when Princess Elizabeth became Queen, engulfed in a tidal wave of New Elizabethan joy — and merchandising. That Dinky Coronation coach we lost the next time we moved is now a prized collectable.

But, of course, the Coronation only came about as a result of the passing away of the Queen's father, King George VI, who died of cancer at Sandringham on 6th February the previous year.

Margaret Stafford recalls:

I grew up in the Sunderland Road area of Gateshead. On the day of the funeral of King George VI, the staff and pupils of King Edward Street School gathered in the hall to listen to the service on the wireless. Our teacher explained the reason for the two minutes' silence and I really did pray for him during that period. We felt very close to our Royal family. We listened to the bulletins about the King's life drawing peacefully to an end, and many tears were shed at the news of his death. Then we started preparing for the Coronation.

But Paul Benneson of Bristol grew up in the Fenlands and experienced the King's death more vividly than if he had been given the news over the wireless:

February is as cold and damp a month as one can get in the Fens. On this day it seemed particularly so. The entire family, consisting of Grandad, Gran, Mum, Dad, my sister and myself, set off to pay our respects to the dead King as the train with his body passed through the Fens on its way to London. Every rail crossing was surrounded by hundreds of people, there to pay their last respects.

The King had died at Sandringham a few days earlier. Everyone seemed to have something black on and the sorrow of the occasion hung about like the damp Fenland mists, heavy and clinging. We waited near the level crossing just outside the village of Streatham and it appeared that the entire village had turned out for the event. The crowd grew but was silent, adding to the sombre atmosphere.

At last the train was spotted coming out of the mist from the direction of Ely. Something alerted the crowd and with a steady and unusually orderly movement everyone moved towards the crossing gates. Small children were lifted onto shoulders, women and the infirm were allowed to the front; and still the crowd was silent. Tears started to flow quietly from many eyes. Memories of the war that had finished only five years earlier perhaps rose and then dimmed.

The train proceeded at a very slow pace for the entire journey, no more than 15 or 20 miles an hour, so that the entire nation could bow their heads. The train itself was dressed overall in black silk. The locomotive, tender, coaches and even the guard's van, were also covered in black. As the train appeared, looming out of the mist, it seemed to me as a young child the most awe-inspiring thing I had ever witnessed. The crowd pressed noiselessly yet firmly on the crossing gates as the train got even nearer. Although it was a steam train it seemed to whisper its way across the misty Fens. When the train passed through the level crossing a single cry of "God Save the King" was heard, the only audible human sound made.

Having passed through the crossing the crowd stood and watched the train disappear into the mist on its way to Cambridge and beyond. With their respects paid, the crowd went slowly and sombrely back from whence they came. As if by magic the atmosphere seemed to have lightened with the passing of the next train. Maybe it was just the end of one era and the start of the new queen's reign, I don't know. All that I am sure of is that it was one of the most powerful experiences of my early life. Such are the emotions and loyalty out of which empires are made.

The ho-ho-ho-ing Edward Heath and the pipe-smoking Harold Wilson dominated politics in Britain in the sixties. Gone were the days of Sir Winston Churchill, who died in 1965 at the age of 91. He had been succeeded as Prime Minister by Anthony Eden, Harold 'You've Never Had It So Good' Macmillan and Alec Douglas-Home before the rivalry of Heath and Wilson, which helped make politics that bit more interesting to the teenager. Politics in the sixties contained some lively and controversial characters like George Brown and Enoch Powell, who was constantly banging the immigration drum. And of course scandals hit a succession of governments, one of the worst being the resignation in 1963 of John Profumo, Harold Macmillan's Secretary of State for War, after his alleged impropriety with Christine Keeler.

In the United States John F Kennedy became the nation's first Roman Catholic leader when elected thirty-fifth President in 1960. He became a well-loved figure, particularly with the youth of America, but his life was also surrounded in controversy and scandal. Sadly JFK was gunned down while travelling in the Presidential limousine through the streets of Dallas on 22nd November 1963. It is said everyone remembers what they were doing when they heard of the assassination.

Sarah Rainford of Cumberland had different priorities:

Being born in 1957 my early recollections of growing up and experiencing life start in the early sixties. Living in a small village in the Lake District, then in the county of Cumberland, life was very simple, quiet and sheltered. The names of Kennedy and Wilson meant little to me. Sindy dolls, roller skates and French skipping were more the thing. The latest issue of Bunty, or the day they introduced flavoured crisps caused more excitement and upheaval than Kennedy's assassination.

The sixties was a grim era of assassinations and, to make it a nightmare decade for the Kennedy family, Senator Robert Kennedy was gunned down in the ballroom of the Embassy Hotel, Los Angeles, on 5th June 1968. Only two months earlier, Civil Rights campaigner Martin Luther King had been ruthlessly shot down on the balcony of the Lorraine Motel, Memphis.

Catherine Bailey of Birmingham recalls:

Assassinations of famous people seemed commonplace in America. I was glad to live in England.

We still played brides, and mummies and daddies (and best of all we played doctors and nurses). The future as far as we could tell was at a neatly ordered time and place perpetuated in the pages of **Look and Learn.**

The advent of mass television in the fifties meant that glittering occasions were enjoyed by the whole nation, and not just those who lived in the capital. The wedding of Princess Margaret and Tony Armstrong-Jones in 1960 was a great occasion.

For some it was only a great occasion because it meant a day off school, as Fiona Carter of Maidstone recalls:

I remember sitting glued to the television thinking how lovely she looked and wouldn't it be nice if I could be a Princess one day. My older brother was out playing football in the street, he didn't go for "cissy" things like that. He was just glad of the day off school. Mind you, I got a bit fed up after about half an hour or so and joined my mates in the street where we all pretended to be Princess Margaret. We couldn't get the boys to join in.

GOLDEN DAYS OF SPORT

Sport and television went arm-in-arm, and what glorious decades the fifties and sixties were for British sports fans.

Memorable moments in the fifties included Roger Bannister breaking the magical four minute barrier for the mile at Iffley Road, Oxford, on 6th May 1954. He achieved this record during an athletics match at Oxford between the Amateur Athletics Association and the University of Oxford. The previous year jockey Gordon Richards won his one and only Derby on Pinza after countless years of trying, and a few weeks earlier Stanley Matthews won his elusive FA Cup winners' medal in one of Wembley's greatest finals.

Colin Devonport lived in Liverpool at the time of Bannister's record-breaking mile, but if he saw it once he saw it a hundred times . . .

I was only six or seven when Bannister broke the world mile record. It didn't mean a lot to me at the time but I'll never forget it — it was on the television all the time. Every time they had four minutes to spare (everything wasn't timed to precision like today) they'd slot it in. I'll never forget him collapsing into that man's arms at the end of the race. They showed it more times than they showed the potter's wheel . . .

The sixties was also a great sporting era. The Rome Olympics were the first to get universal television coverage and in 1966 the England soccer team captured the hearts of the British people when they beat West Germany 4-2 after extra time to win the World Cup on home soil.

It was a joyous occasion but a few months earlier the famous Jules Rimet trophy went missing whilst on display at Westminster's Central Hall. Scotland Yard failed to find the trophy; that task was left to a black and white mongrel called Pickles.

Rob White lived in Burnley at the time of the World Cup:

I was an avid Burnley supporter, they were in the first division at the time. The World Cup really stirred our imaginations and me and my mates were really rooting for them. It was a great moment when the final whistle went and then Bobby Moore held up the trophy. I felt proud to be English. I never thought England would win the World Cup but there again I never thought Burnley would ever be in the fourth division!

There were other important events taking place while the world was either at war, encountering disasters, enjoying weddings or revelling in sporting achievements.

Mount Everest was conquered for the first time when Edmund Hillary and Sherpa Tenzing reached the summit on 31st May 1953. Ten years later there was the daredevil robbery of a Glasgow to London mail train by the Great Train Robbers which ultimately resulted in lengthy prison sentences for many of its culprits, including men who have since become cult figures – Ronnie Biggs, the late Charles Wilson, Buster Edwards and so on.

The list of technological advancements in the fifties and sixties was never ending as Britain came out of its wartime depression to provide a new life for the teenagers of the seventies, eighties and nineties.

Edward Rainford from what was the County of Westmoreland:

Our black and white television set was very temperamental; the valve was constantly blowing, leaving a dark sooty mark up the wall.

I don't have any recollection of adverts in between programmes, just those wonderful BBC voices giving details of repairs to local transmitters. And of course the disappearing dot when the set was switched off. With the colour set came the familiar "Test Card" of the girl with the teddy bear.

At the beginning of the fifties television was a 20th century marvel enjoyed by a minority. 20 years later nearly every household had a set; furthermore, viewers could get three channels and enjoy pictures in colour. Computers gradually became part of everyday life, instead of something people only read about, and by the end of the sixties they played a key role in putting man on the moon. Man's landing on the moon's surface, at 3.56 a.m. BST on 21st July 1969, was the most significant world event since the day Christ was born.

Architecture came a long way and the fifties saw an increasing number of tower blocks to help the inner city housing problems. However, they also created major problems, as was evident when part of the Ronan Point block in London's docklands area collapsed like a deck of cards in 1968. Mercifully, there were few deaths but the disaster highlighted the dangers of such towering buildings. Nevertheless, architects still went ahead and the craze for high-rise structures was further highlighted by the Post Office Tower and Harry Hyams' 34-storey Centre Point building in the heart of London's West End.

Patricia Simms, now a mother of three teenagers:

When I look at what my kids have got: colour television, videos, compact disc players, satellite dishes, cars at 18 and a never-ending flow of money, I often think back to "the good old days" when all we had was friendship. But were they really the good old days, I sometimes ask myself when I look at the world around me today? But I'm glad I grew up in the fifties and sixties.

The children of today take computers, television, space flight and ugly concrete structures for granted. But, as we have seen, some families didn't even have electricity, running water or an inside loo at the beginning of the fifties. We have come a long way since then.

ACKNOWLEDGMENTS

Trevor Dolby *Managing Editor*

The Author

The Publishers would like to thank the following organisations and individuals for their kind permission to reproduce the photographs in this book.

Associated Press 126 left; © BBC 74 top; The Design Museum 66 bottom, 69 left; © Fleetway Publications 1990 101 top left; Duffpix International 117 bottom; Fuzzy Felt, Allan Industries Ltd. 96 top; Abram Games 111 bottom left, 113 top right, /© BBC 71 top left; Dianne Gatford 111 bottom right; The Girl Guides Association 104 left, top right and bottom right; Ronald Grant Archive 106 top, bottom left and bottom right, 107 inset, 123 inset, 137 bottom; The Hulton Picture Company 2, 9, 12, 13 right, 15, 20 bottom, 28 left, 30, 34-5, 40, 43, 45, 46 bottom, 47, 48-9, 50-1, 51, 52 bottom, 54, 56, 56-7, 57, 58, 59, 60, 66 top, 66-7, 67, 70 main, 71 top right, 72-3, 75 top and bottom, 77 left, 79, 81, 82, 83, 84, 85, 86 inset, 86-7, 87 inset, 88 bottom, 89, 90, 91 bottom, 92-3, 93 inset, 94, 95 top right, 97 left, top right and bottom right, 98 left, 100 left and right, 101 top right, 116, 117 top, 121, 124 inset, 124-5, 125 inset, 128-9, 129 right, 133 left and right, 136, 137 top, 138 inset, 138-9, 142, 143, 145 inset, 146 left, 149, 153, 155; Kinemacollection 102; London Features International 141 top; 'Meccano Everything' Henley-on-Thames (The Meccano name is copyright of Meccano, Calais) 95 bottom left, 114, 151; Nick Nicholson 88 top, 95 top left and bottom right, 96 bottom, 99 centre and bottom, 101 bottom, 103 top left and top right, 107, 109 bottom; James Nisbet & Co. Ltd/Mabel O'Donnell & Rona Munro 26 right; Octopus Group Picture Library/Howell Evans 26 left, 68, /Feature Photography 158, /DT Grewcock 27, /Suzanne Szasz 41 right; The Robert Opie Collection 11, 17, 46 top, 48 inset, 52 top, 53 top, bottom left and bottom right, 61 top and centre, 62, 63 top and bottom right, 64, 69 bottom right, 70 inset, 71 bottom, 72 inset, 73 inset, 74 bottom, 76, 91 top, 98 right, 99 top left and top right, 103 bottom left and bottom right, 108 bottom left, 109 top, 111 top, 112 top left, 115 inset, 127 top, 140 top, 141 bottom, 155 top and centre, /© Fleetway Publications 1990 69 centre right, 108 right, /© D C Thomson & Co. Ltd. 108 top left and centre left; Popperfoto Endpapers 16, 23, 25, 28-9, 29 right, 31, 32-3, 35 bottom, 37, 39, 41 left, 110, 112-3, 115, 130, 135, 153 inset, 154, 157; Retrograph Archive, London 55 top and bottom, 61 bottom, /James Robertson & Sons 63 bottom left, 65, 74 centre, 77 right; The Scout Association 105 top and bottom; Chris Tarrant 14, 20 top; Topham Picture Library 8-9, 10, 13 left, 18, 36, 38, 119, 123, 127 bottom, 128 left, 131, 132, 133, 134, 140 bottom left and bottom right, 144 inset, 144-5, 146 right, 147.

Although every effort has been made to trace the copyright holder, we apologise in advance for any unintentional omissions and would be pleased to insert the appropriate acknowledgments in any subsequent edition of this publication.

Captions Trevor Dolby, Philip Dodd, Carolyn Pyrah.

Text set in 10pt Trade Gothic by Dorchester Typesetting.

Jane McIntosh *Editor*

Philip Dodd *Publisher*

Nick Thompson *Production*

Carolyn Pyrah *Editor*

Emily Hedges *Picture Research*